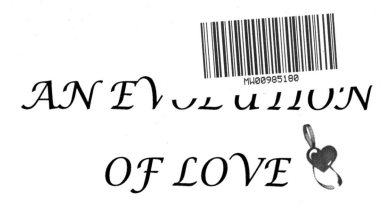

# AN EVOLUTION
# OF LOVE

Life and Love with Frontotemporal Dementia

## ROBERT JAMES SYKES, JR.

### A MEMOIR

### MARIE SYKES
### MICHELLE STAFFORD

**Photo Credits:**

Professional Portraits: PCA International, Inc., 815 Matthews–Mint Hill Rd., Matthews, North Carolina 28105. Page 3 and 29 - All Rights Reserved


Goofy © Disney Enterprises, Inc. Page 117
Used by permission from Disney Enterprises, Inc.


**Cover Credits:**

Design - Michelle Stafford. Color Assistant – Dave Rucker

ISBN: **978-0-615-15449-7**

**Georgetown Publishing, LLC**

PO Box 324
Langhorne, PA 19047


**Order Online at:**
www.AnEvolutionOfLove.com

*In loving memory of our wonderful husband and father,*

# *Robert James Sykes, Jr.*

January 23, 1956 – April 7, 2006

# CONTENTS

# Acknowledgements

We would like to thank our Associate Writer, Orlo Otteson. From our first conversation, Orlo captured the spirit of this project, and he worked diligently to maintain our voice and to faithfully tell our story.

We also want to express our sincere appreciation to our Copy Editors, Kate Mattson and Patti Levenberg. Their friendship and willingness to assist us by sharing their time and talent has helped us to shape our manuscript into a cohesive memoir. Kate and Patti's attention to detail while proofreading and editing our manuscript from the reader's perspective was invaluable.

We want to thank our talented website designer, Gary Kovar, for developing a site that reflects our vision. His expertise and personal interest in our venture was priceless.

-Marie Sykes and Michelle Stafford

*B*ob, Michelle, and I have been blessed by the outpouring of love and support we received throughout Bob's illness and our heartbreak. Knowing that so many people cared about us, and prayed for us, and wanted to "do something to help," gave us the strength to survive.

A special thank you to my dear daughter, Michelle, for being the loving, thoughtful, caring person she is. Where do I begin? She is my guardian angel here on earth. I don't know how I would have ever survived this difficult journey without her love, support, dedication, and patience. I can't imagine any other mother being more proud of her daughter than I am of Michelle.

I want to thank Dr. Lewis Dunn, our family's Primary Care Physician. Dr. Dunn's genuine concern and caring ways were invaluable. He was very patient with Bob during office visits, and he remains a source of support for Michelle and me, as we grieve the loss of Bob.

I also want to thank Dr. Ronny Antelo, Neurologist, who quickly recognized Bob's Frontotemporal Dementia. Dr. Antelo is a caring, kind, and helpful gentleman. He was available to me by phone any time, day or night. He respected Bob's dignity and showed great kindness, while also expressing genuine concern for Michelle and me. I will always remember one special office visit. Michelle had taken Bob out of the examining room, giving Dr. Antelo and me a few minutes to talk. During that conversation, Dr. Antelo told me that I had his "complete admiration," and he said that I was a "hero" in the way I accepted and handled Bob's disease. Those supportive words from a man I trust and admire overwhelmed me.

Another important person to thank is Betty Moran-Organ, Director of the Sunrise at Floral Vale Assisted Living Community where Bob spent the last nine months of his life. Betty willingly accepted Bob into their home, when others would not. Bob's relatively young age, together with his mobility, presented challenges other facilities were not prepared to accept. Betty listened to my concerns and worked with me to resolve them. She took a personal interest in Bob, and immediately came to the hospital when Bob was moved to the Intensive Care Unit. I cried on her shoulder the moment I saw her. Betty is a very caring person, and she will always hold a special place in my heart.

I've asked myself many times, how can I possibly thank everyone who helped Bob, Michelle, and me through this difficult journey? How do we properly and completely extend our thanks and appreciation to so many people? To family and friends, I simply say, Thank You. Your love, prayers, and support have been more helpful than words can express. I hope you know how grateful we are to each and everyone of you. Thanks for all you have done for each of us.

Finally, I thank God for His Love. He continues to bless me, while helping me to start each day with a new attitude and a sense of gratitude.

-*Marie Sykes*

# Preface

This book is a tribute to a beloved husband and a loving father, Robert James Sykes, Jr. We have written this book as a way of preserving Bob's memory and capturing the spirit of this special man, who left us too soon and is sorely missed.

In December 2003, at the age of 47, Bob was diagnosed with Frontotemporal Dementia (FTD), a brain disease that slowly erodes cognitive abilities and causes personality changes. He endured the disease for more than three years, finally succumbing on April 7, 2006. Working with my daughter Michelle, I have tried to describe Bob's courageous attempts to cope with this progressive, irreversible disease. We have also tried to communicate the caregiving complexities associated with the disease and the ways in which one family coped with a heartbreaking dementia experience.

Most of all, however, we have strived to paint a picture of a unique individual, a generous and giving man, who selflessly devoted himself to our family life. It is a story of loss, but it is also a story of love and devotion in the face of devastating illness. We hope this story will provide support and inspiration to others who are coping with dementia and other irreversible illnesses.

Bob's illness (FTD) causes personality changes, and the effects, especially before diagnosis, can be devastating. Throughout the illness, I felt the loss of my husband many times and in several ways. At the beginning, Bob seemed to distance himself from me, a behavior I attributed to a relationship problem. Diagnosis brought some relief; at least I could name the problem. As the disease progressed, Bob steadily withdrew, and I wholeheartedly felt the loss of a great companion. I then experienced the need to transition into the role of caregiver, and I was required to attend to Bob in ways that one would attend to a child. I mourned the loss of my husband in the sense of my partner, best friend, and pillar. Then, after Bob moved into Assisted Living, I had to adjust to an empty house and to the loss of his presence.

At one point in the illness, Michelle and I began to differentiate between "Old Bob," the Bob we knew before the illness, and "New Bob," the Bob afflicted with a dreadful disease. We found this coping mechanism to be a useful tool in helping us relate to Bob and in maintaining our sense of who he once was—a strong, capable, responsible man. We knew that the disease had robbed us of the "Old Bob," but we grew to love and appreciate the "New Bob." We cherished each moment we were able to spend with him.

When family and friends paid their respects at Bob's viewing and memorial service, I often repeated the same sentiment. "We never expected to lose Bob this soon, but dementia strips a person of dignity, and Bob was no exception. If he had lived longer, he would have lost even more of what made him special. I feel God spared Bob from having to endure more loss, and He also spared Bob's loved ones from having to watch this happen."

Those thoughts and feelings, together with my faith in God, have given me strength and comfort. The dementia experience has been described as "a long goodbye." Truer words cannot be spoken. I now feel the ultimate loss, but I also recall the wonderful gifts that Bob gave to me and Michelle. This book describes some of those gifts, and as Bob watches down from Heaven above, I pray this memoir is a tribute that he, too, can be proud of. It is a labor of love and a gift to the man I love deep in my heart.

-*Marie Sykes*

# CHAPTER ONE

# ROBERT JAMES SYKES, JR.

## The Beginning

Robert James Sykes, Jr., was born on January 23, 1956, on a cold, wintry, Philadelphia day. His father, Bob Sykes Sr., a second-year seminarian, had returned home from class the previous day to be greeted with some big news. "Today," said his expectant and fully pregnant wife, Mary, "might be The Day."

A light snow had begun to fall, and Mary, growing a bit apprehensive and unwilling to take chances, asked her brother Bill for a ride to a hospital. Bob and Mary had not yet bought a car and Bill, eager to help, quickly responded. Medical facilities were crowded, however, and the search for a hospital proved a bit difficult.

Mary was finally admitted, and at 4:00 a.m. on a snowy, Thursday morning, Bob Jr. arrived—the beginning of a family that would eventually include Kathy, Tom, John, and Steve. Bob Sr. and Mary warmly welcomed and embraced all of their children as they came along, but Bob Jr., being the first-born, seemed to always hold a special place in family life, and he enjoyed his "big brother" role.

Bob spent his first two years in an apartment in the Wissinoming section of Philadelphia, Pennsylvania. The family then moved to Woodbury, New Jersey, where his father assumed a Rector's position and where his sister Kathy and brother Tom were born. In 1960, the family moved to Berlin, New Jersey, where they spent the next ten years.

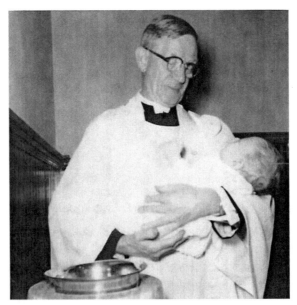

*Rev. Gillespie & Bob Jr.*
*April 1956*

## Berlin Days

Bob spent his pre-school years in the usual childhood pursuits, often playing with his sister Kathy in the large back yard. In 1962, he entered Berlin Elementary School, which housed grades one through eight. The school had received a federal grant to establish special programs in the social studies and science areas, and Bob eagerly participated in these educational activities.

*Bob with a prize winning school project*

Tom remembers sharing bunks in their small Berlin bedroom and going over each day's events. Tom also recalls when heavy snow days provided the possibility of a school closing. Bob would throw open the window, withstand the blast of cold air, and listen for the fire siren—a signal that the school day had been cancelled.

Outside of school, Bob and his friend Dave spent hours together, riding their bikes around town, performing errands, and catching fish and chasing tadpoles at Berlin Park. Bob loved the outdoors.

Bob's love of the outdoors was inspired by the family's vacations, which included camping trips on the Bass River. The family often enjoyed summer swims in Lake Absegami and hikes up to the Fire Tower.

*Bob, Tom & Kathy on a family camping trip in New Hampshire*

Bob also enjoyed Boy Scout activities, which included summer camping excursions. One Boy Scout camping experience stands out. Bob forgot to bring along his pajamas. So, he asked his father to deliver a pair of pajamas to the campground. That evening Bob became "sick"—an illness his brother Tom forever believed was brought on by the mocking of fellow scouts. What kind of rugged scout has his father deliver a pair of pajamas? Bob Sr. picked up his young son at camp and delivered him from further embarrassment.

Canoeing was also a favorite pastime, and the Bass River in the Pine Barrens of South Jersey provided special pleasures. Following one canoe outing, several scouts decided to take a dip in the river, not knowing the ways in which cedar and pine trees had affected the water's composition. Bob Sr. remembered, "They went into the water white as snow; they came out dark as toast." The stains finally came out but only after days of scrubbing.

Bob expressed his love for nature in his own backyard. He enjoyed growing flowers, which he sometimes placed in his father's church, and vegetables, which found their way to the family dinner table. At one point in these early years, he and his grandfather Hoehn planted fruit trees in back of his grandparents' house. To everyone's amazement, the trees actually produced some fruit. Later on, grandfather Hoehn planted a blue spruce tree on the side churchyard. Bob tended it and family members watched it grow. The nearby family house eventually disappeared, but the beautiful, twenty-five foot, spruce tree still stands, a living monument to Bob.

The backyard was a gathering spot for the neighborhood kids. Bob, now called "Big Bob," by his friends, found himself at the center of these backyard activities. He also enjoyed playing board games like chess and Stratego, and through these games he began to exhibit the analytical skills that would propel his professional career. The New Jersey days would end, however, and a new chapter would begin.

## Rockledge Days

In 1968, at the end of Bob's sixth grade school year, his father accepted a call to serve as Rector of Holy Nativity church in Rockledge, Pennsylvania—a big move for Bob Jr., who was about to enter junior high school and was understandably reluctant to leave friends and familiar surroundings.

Bob started seventh grade in Rockledge, and music began to enter into his life—ELO, Mike Oldfield, Bruce Springsteen were favorites. Church youth activities also provided ongoing pleasure and stimulation, and Bob even did an acting turn, playing King Herod in a production of *Jesus Christ Superstar*.

During his years at Abington High School, Bob became deeply involved with the school radio station, serving as one of its first DJs. This interest continued on through his college years. Moreover, he began to develop a strong interest in accounting, and under the guiding hand of his Uncle Bill, a CPA, young Bob firmly determined that he would prepare for an accounting career.

*John, Kathy, Steve, Bob and Tom*

Bob's interest in accounting continued at Drexel University. During summers, as part of a work-study program, he worked in the office of a clothing manufacturer, a bank, and a CPA firm. Bob graduated from Drexel University in 1979 with a degree in Business Administration. He would later spend twelve years with AAA Mid-Atlantic, working as a Programmer Analyst. At the onset of his illness, Bob was pursuing a Master of Science Degree in Computer Information Science at LaSalle University.

Bob as a DJ for Drexel University

# CHAPTER TWO

# FTD —THE DISEASE

## Frontotemporal Dementia (FTD): An Overview

To understand Bob's struggle, one must first understand the nature of his illness—*Frontotemporal Dementia*. This form of dementia (there are approximately 55 different types) typically strikes adults at a relatively early age. Patients do not usually experience memory loss in the early stages, unlike Alzheimer's patients. Over the first few years, they are able to maintain language and visual perception capabilities. Ultimately, however, changes in personality become evident. Individuals lose social skills and reasoning powers. Motivation and concentration abilities wane, and individuals stop relating, socially and emotionally, in usual ways. Since brain degeneration is not widespread in this early stage, afflicted individuals generally retain memory function. The disease, however, begins to attack brain areas that control reasoning, judgment, and the ability to take initiative.

The brain abnormalities take two forms. The first type, called *non-specific focal degeneration*, accounts for eighty percent of FTD cases. These cases are called "non-specific" because autopsies show no identifiable abnormal particles —only evidence of reduced brain cells. The second type, called *Pick's disease*, accounts for the other twenty percent of FTD cases. In these cases, abnormal particles, called "Pick bodies", begin to occupy the brain.

## Comportment, Insight, Reasoning

Frontotemporal Dementia affects the part of the brain that regulates *comportment*, *insight*, and *reasoning*.

**Comportment** is a term that refers to social behavior, insight skills, and appropriateness. It involves the ability to conduct one's self in socially acceptable ways and to adjust behavior. Conventional behavior at a funeral, for example, differs from accepted behavior at a birthday party.

Comportment problems are difficult to deal with. FTD victims exhibit personality changes. A generally active individual may become apathetic and withdrawn, whereas, a usually reserved individual may become disinhibited, outgoing, and/or boisterous. These personality changes may express themselves in increased levels of irritability and anger, emotions that can lead to occasional outbursts, sometimes physical in nature and usually directed at a caregiver.

**Insight** is another element of comportment, which relates to the ability to see one's self as others do and to act in socially acceptable and reasonable ways. Insight also relates to an individual's ability to recognize his or her deficits and illness symptoms. A decline in insight abilities leads to inappropriate behaviors.

***Reasoning*** is a critical human skill that refers to mental activities which promote effective decision-making. FTD patients frequently show reasoning deficits, for example, an inability to categorize information and to see problems from various perspectives. They also lose the ability to organize and plan the flow of behavior. In an emergency (a car accident, for example), an FTD patient might have difficulty handling all the stimulation of the moment and might not be able to adequately respond.

Frontotemporal Dementia individuals lose thinking flexibility and the ability to complete projects. They lose the ability to plan appropriate actions or to cease inappropriate actions; all of which can lead to risky behaviors.

The Feinberg School of Medicine at Northwestern University has assembled a summary of FTD symptoms:

- ***Impairments in social skills***: inappropriate or bizarre social behavior (e.g., eating with one's fingers, overly familiar interaction with strangers).

- ***Changes in activity levels***: apathy, withdrawal, reduced motivation and initiative. These are often symptoms of psychological depression but in this case not necessarily accompanied by feelings of sadness.

- ***Decreased judgment***: impairments in financial decision-making (e.g., impulsive spending), difficulty in recognizing consequences of behavior and inability to understand threats to personal safety (e. g., inviting strangers into the house).

- ***Changes in personal habits***: poor personal appearance, irresponsible actions and compulsive behaviors (e.g., need to engage in repetitive actions).

*Alterations in personality and mood*: increased irritability and decreased ability to tolerate frustration.

*Changes in customary emotional responsiveness*: loss of sympathetic or compassionate responses and heightened emotionality.

Everyone requires attention, concentration, and the ability to organize information for successful mental activity. Frontal lobe dementia impairs all these specific functions and gravely affects normal behavior. When undiagnosed, relationships and family life seriously erode.

Frontotemporal Dementia poses special psychological, social, family, and financial problems—issues that frequently differ in nature from those associated with Alzheimer's type dementia. FTD strikes relatively early in life, often at a time when an individual is dealing with career challenges and family demands. Many afflicted individuals have not approached retirement age, and the impairment can seriously jeopardize the family's financial position and overall security. The nature of the symptoms can lead to a loss of friendships and social support. Moreover, most adult day programs and residential care facilities are not fully equipped to address the special needs of the younger, non-Alzheimer's patient, especially if the behavioral symptoms prove difficult and demanding.

These first two chapters have given the fundamental facts about Bob's life and the nature of FTD, but they say little about the character of this beloved son, brother, husband, and father. They also communicate little about the wrenching pain that accompanied Bob's pre-diagnostic period.

The "Old Bob" (the capable man who existed before the onset of FTD) and the emerging "New Bob"(the afflicted individual beginning to exhibit puzzling behaviors) are best described by his loving wife, Marie, his faithful partner for eighteen years.

# CHAPTER THREE

## OLD BOB—NEW BOB

With progressive, dementing illness, the prediagnosis phase is marked by the family's uncertainty and ambivalence. The onset of Frontotemporal Dementia and its insidious entry into family life raises difficult questions.

- Are certain worrisome symptoms signs of psychiatric disorder or early signs of a dementing illness?
- Should we be concerned, or should we leave well enough alone for now?
- Should we discuss our concerns with friends and other family members? If so, with whom?
- Should we discuss our concerns with our "affected" loved one? If so, when and how?

Family uncertainty in this phase is fueled by *ambiguity* (difficulty in knowing) and *ambivalence* (difficulty in deciding). Ongoing uncertainty holds the potential for undermining family coping efforts and disorganizing family life.

*Marie*: *I was a single parent to my daughter, Michelle; from the time she was a twenty-month-old toddler. We were a family unit, and we were close. During Michelle's pre-school years, I could not afford day care services, but Michelle received great attention from my mother and from my sister, Lynn, whose two young children provided needed companionship.*

*Bob and I met at work. We both worked in separate areas of the Information Services Department at Reliance Standard Life Insurance Company. I had worked there for four years before Bob joined the team in July 1985. A year later, the company developed its own onsite data center. I was given the job of Tape Librarian. Bob was assigned to select an offsite storage facility for the tapes. Bob identified three possible sites and the two of us scheduled visits to each location.*

*During the rides to and from these sites, I began to see Bob in a different light. At the office, he was seen as a hard worker and something of a character, fun loving and witty, although always gentle with his humor and well respected. In our car-ride conversations, he came across as personable, gracious, sentimental, and highly family oriented. I learned that Bob's father, a former Episcopalian minister, now worked as a nurse at Norristown State Hospital, and I discovered Bob's close attachment to his family members.*

*Bob and I worked diligently to evaluate and make a recommendation for an offsite tape storage solution. Soon we began "running" into each other in the cafeteria before the work day started and finding ways to converse. We began dating shortly after the project ended and the relationship steadily deepened.*

*On April 16, 1988, Bob and I were married in All Saints Episcopal Church in Philadelphia, Pennsylvania. Bob's father officiated. Michelle was not quite twelve years old.*

*Our Wedding – April 16, 1988*

## Old Bob

Marie recalls the "Old Bob"—the Bob she knew before the onset of the devastating disease, Frontotemporal Dementia.

**Marie:** *Bob was a very intelligent man. My mother used to say that he knew a little bit about everything. He was an excellent role model for Michelle. He led by example, and he* *was very proud of Michelle and me and of our accomplishments.*

*Bob was always very sentimental. He remembered every occasion and saved every card I ever gave him. On the six-month anniversary of our first date, Bob sent me six roses, followed by a dozen roses on our first anniversary. He loved sending me roses. He would send flowers on special occasions, but he loved to surprise me by sending them just because.*

*Bob also liked to give me cards containing handwritten notes. He constantly expressed his love for me. A year or two before his illness, Bob sent me flowers on HIS birthday, with a note thanking me for sharing in his life.*

*Bob was patient and thoughtful, and had a big and warm heart. He was detail oriented and organized. Bob was fun, and taught me to laugh at myself. He was loving, giving, and always supportive of Michelle and me. Bob lived by the sentiment, 'All I want in life, Marie, is for you to be happy. When you're happy, I'm happy.'*

*Bob had the patience of a saint. His needs were simple; he was not a materialistic person. Bob was family oriented, and he doted on us. When we got the munchies, he'd think nothing of going out for Slurpees, donuts, brownies, all kinds of treats.*

*Everything Bob did he did from the heart, with no strings attached. Nothing was too much trouble, and he was happy to do for others. He was honest, trustworthy, and reliable. He had a zest for life.*

*Moreover, Bob was not a typical man. If a button needed to be sewn onto a shirt, Bob got out needle and thread and sewed it on himself. He cleaned the house, and he did a great job. He knew when to change the sheets and flip the mattress. He balanced the checkbook and kept track of our savings and investment programs.*

*Bob loved to garden; he grew flowers and the best tomatoes around. He didn't even like tomatoes! Bob liked to grow them and give them away to people who enjoyed them. His generous nature was always on display.*

*Bob loved to read and he frequently had several books going at a time. He enjoyed taking photographs during vacation trips and at family functions. He was an avid Star Trek fan, an interest Michelle and I did not share.*

*Bob also loved to spend time with Michelle and me. We regularly went out to Friday night dinners. The three of us enjoyed attending Broadway musicals and Philadelphia Phillies baseball games. We traveled to Disney World several times, Niagara Falls, Mystic CT, Williamsburg VA, the Bahamas, London, and took a cruise to Bermuda. We never tired of one another's company.*

**Bob and Michelle before one of Michelle's softball games – Spring 1988**

*Bob was a morning person. He was always pleasant and sometimes could be heard whistling while getting ready for work. Michelle and I didn't always appreciate this morning happiness. Bob would wake up at 5:00 a.m., take his shower, and then try to gently wake me. I was not a morning person, but I would finally get to my feet, and then, after taking a shower, I would find a cup of tea waiting for me in the bedroom. As Bob awaited my arrival downstairs, he would go through the morning paper. Then, often running a little late (my fault), we would set off to work. I always knew that the lunch bag I'd prepared for myself the evening before would be sitting on the car seat.*

Marie, Michelle and Bob – February 2002

*Bob also retained fond memories of his childhood days. He would recount details of his boy scout camping days and his experience growing up in the church. As a child, he earned a little spending money grooming the church grounds and performing other needed tasks. He also liked to recall times he'd spent with Grandfather Hoehn and Grandfather Sykes, planting vegetable gardens and developing an interest in model trains. The train interest turned into a life-long avocation. Bob also spent childhood days with his Aunt Sarah and Uncle Russ and their children. He often talked about the responsibility he felt as "Big Bob" to keep a watchful eye on his younger siblings. Bob's childhood was a happy one, and as an adult, he communicated a sense of happiness about who he was.*

## New Bob

Contrast this picture of the "Old Bob" with the slow-motion, horror film that began to develop, as Frontotemporal Dementia began to take its terrible toll.

> **Marie**: *In early 2002, Bob started to become distant and withdrawn. He became easily fatigued and he lost interest in his hobbies. Bob's appetite declined, and he lost weight, while also developing an uncharacteristic appetite for sweets. His priorities seemed to shift. His interest in our relationship and in his work seemed to slide away.*

> *Looking back, Michelle and I think that we first noticed a subtle personality change around December 2000, on a family vacation to Disney World. He was quiet and reserved, not his usual outgoing, pleasant self. One day, while we were being transported to one of the parks by a Walt Disney World bus, his face took on a distant look, and his eyes filled with tears. This didn't make any sense to us. This was Bob's favorite vacation spot, yet he didn't seem to be enjoying himself. When we would ask if something was wrong, he'd say, 'No, everything is fine.'*

> *One time, when Michelle was still living at home, she took two of my great-nephews to The Crayola Factory for the day. The boys then spent the night at our house. The next morning, while*

*we were eating breakfast and preparing for church services, I noticed the older of the two boys, Dominick, looking at Bob, who was sitting alone in the living room and staring into space. Dominick asked me, 'What's Uncle Bob doing?' I replied, 'Oh, he's just sitting.' Dominick said, 'It looks like he's staring at the wall.' I said, 'Yes, he does that sometimes.' Dominick asked, 'Why?' I answered him honestly. 'I really don't know why.' Dominick looked puzzled. At this point, even a seven year old child could detect Bob's unusual behavior.*

## The FTD Symptoms Steadily Worsen

**Marie**: *At the time that Bob was undergoing these personality and cognitive changes, he was also pursuing a Master of Science Degree in Computer Information Science at LaSalle University, Bucks County Campus. When he finished his last class in December 2002, he had compiled a 3.8 GPA. I can only imagine how hard he must have worked as he struggled to compensate for the crippling effects of an undiagnosed illness.*

*Bob was working as a Computer Programmer and Business Analyst. He was a very conscientious person, a hard worker who took pride in his abilities. When the personality changes became even more noticeable, I began to worry about his job performance and security. Sadly, my fears were soon confirmed. On January 22, 2003, Bob's employer suspended him for a day and placed him on ninety days probation.*

*Bob was in denial about the work issue. He blamed the problems on two new managers, whom he said didn't have programming experience and didn't know the business. Bob felt that they didn't know what they were doing.*

### An Evolution of Love

*Despite the problems at work, Bob's efforts to please me continued. Throughout the disease, before and after the diagnosis, he would always apologize for his uncharacteristic and puzzling behaviors. Prior to the diagnosis, and before I understood the source of his behaviors, I would try to discuss them with Bob, but he would always deny that anything had changed. He would always repeat a familiar refrain, insisting that he loved Michelle and me, and that we were the most important people in his life.*

*I didn't know what was going on. I didn't know why Bob was changing in so many ways and I often felt sad, hurt, angry, and confused. I was at a loss about what to say and how to react. He had distanced himself, and whenever I tried to kiss or hug him, he would freeze. Bob had always been an affectionate husband. He used to love holding my hand, but now when I'd take his hand, he would just gently shake free of my loving grip.*

*I naturally thought this distancing was a sign of marital trouble. I was heartbroken. I thought Bob's feelings toward me had changed and, yet, he still seemed to care about me. It was all confusing and distressing. When I would attempt to talk about the changes I was seeing, he would say, 'You're right, I'm sorry. I'll try harder.'*

*After hearing this over and over, I began to feel that the remarks had become an easy way to avoid responsibility for addressing the issues that so troubled me. He seemed to think that he merely had to say, 'I'm sorry.'*

*My frustration and confusion steadily increased. I found myself becoming angry at times. I had so many emotions, and they all cut so deeply into me. My heart ached. I didn't know why he was behaving so differently. He was evolving into a completely different person. This was not the man I had known and loved for so many years. I had lost my husband and partner. I now know that I'd lost him long before the diagnosis.*

*Bob began obsessively inquiring about Michelle's activities. In the beginning stage of the disease, Michelle was living at home, but she had already graduated from college. She was a young adult, in her early twenties. Bob began to repeatedly inquire into her personal life, which frustrated and irritated Michelle. Bob hadn't asked these kinds of questions when she was a teenager. It didn't make sense to us. I often asked Bob why he questioned Michelle, but he would simply say, 'I just worry about her.'*

*The behavior was especially puzzling in light of Bob's previous history with Michelle. She was ten years old when Bob and I began dating. He worked hard to develop a nurturing relationship with her. She had a relationship with her father at the time, and Bob understood the delicate nature of the circumstances. He was very careful not to interfere in her relationship and not to step on toes. He was extremely sensitive to these kinds of issues, and now it seemed as though that kind of sensitivity had vanished. It was confusing and painful.*

*Deep in my heart, I knew something was wrong. I knew this wasn't the man I had married. At times, I didn't even like him, but I never denied what I was seeing. As time went on, I began to think that Bob had fallen into a deep psychological depression. The extreme fatigue, the appetite loss, and the withdrawal from usual activities seemed to signal depression. I was at a loss. I didn't know what to do. I decided to consult, Dr. Dunn, our primary care physician.*

# CHAPTER FOUR

# TOWARD A DIAGNOSIS

The diagnosis phase is marked by a series of difficult questions.

- When should we seek a diagnosis?
- To whom should we turn?
- What is our role in the diagnostic process?

Family members may understandably shrink from the diagnostic task, turn away from the prospect of confronting a potential dementing illness. In time, however, increasingly apparent problems impel most families to seek medical advice.

> **Marie**: *In November 2002, Bob and I visited our family doctor for a routine checkup. I expressed my concerns to the doctor about Bob's behavioral changes and my frustration with his fatigue and withdrawal. I explained that Bob seemed to*

*spend most of his time in the living room, sometimes sitting in the dark and just staring off into space. I was obviously pained, and the tears streamed freely down my cheeks.*

*The doctor continued to write a prescription for Bob's blood work and then added some additional tests to the script. Some time later, we followed up with the same doctor to discuss the test results. I began to further describe ways in which Bob's personality was changing. The doctor turned to Bob and asked him if he loved me. Bob immediately responded, 'Yes! Marie and Michelle are the most important people in my life.'*

*Bob acknowledged my unhappiness. He said he could see it, but he said he couldn't see any change in our relationship. The doctor advised us to start marriage counseling, which we did, in December 2002.*

*After a few months of counseling, the therapist stated to me that while she couldn't see a problem in our marriage, she sensed a problem she couldn't pinpoint. In the meantime, Bob's behavior continued to change. More and more he would shrug off my complaints with the words, 'I'm sorry, you're right, I'll try harder.' It was all unbelievably frustrating.*

*We began having individual sessions with the counselor. Bob would see her one week; I would see her the next. On a number of occasions, I suggested that Bob should perhaps see a psychiatrist. I thought he might need medication, but the therapist was reluctant to refer Bob to a psychiatrist. She thought a psychiatrist would ask Bob why he was there and that Bob would simply reply, 'Because my wife wanted me to come.'*

*This was the first of many roadblocks I would face. The therapist was acknowledging that something was wrong, while assuring me that Bob loved me and cared about me. I appreciated hearing this, but the words didn't help much. I subsequently aimed some harsh words at the therapist. I accused her of taking Bob's side, of being an enabler. She told me she wasn't taking anyone's side and that she'd never seen a problem like this.*

*I kept pushing for a psychiatric evaluation, and finally the therapist agreed. She referred us to Dr. Rona Cohen, a psychiatrist within the group. Dr. Cohen agreed to evaluate Bob, using background information that had been gathered in the therapy sessions.*

*On July 1, 2003, Bob lost his job, a position he'd held for twelve years. His performance had steadily declined. He was shocked! He couldn't see any change in his performance or behaviors, and he couldn't understand the reasons for the dismissal. I was devastated. I had feared and suspected that termination was coming, but the reality still shocked me. Ironically, Bob's initial evaluation with the psychiatrist occurred the same day.*

*Up to this point, Michelle and I had done our best to hide Bob's changing behaviors. Now that he'd lost his job, however, we had to tell family members and friends about our concerns. Our families were shocked by the news of Bob's termination. I didn't say much about his behavior, other than to note that he seemed depressed.*

Michelle sent a letter to our therapist as summarized below:

I write this letter out of concern for my parents, Marie and Bob Sykes. I feel the need to make sure that you have a clear picture of what is going on, so that you are better able to help them.

Bob has become increasingly withdrawn from all aspects of his life, including hobbies and his relationship with my mother and myself. I have seen him "perk up" when he is in the company of others, especially his parents. Bob spends hours a day alone in a dimly lit room staring at the wall or sleeping. He sleeps excessively and even more so now that he is not working. Bob has no desire to work in the yard, read or do things he used to really enjoy, and he has also lost about thirty pounds without trying. I've seen his judgment diminish over the past several months.

Bob is the reason my mom cries. He is the reason she comes to me asking what she's doing wrong. He is the reason that she fears they will lose their home and that their marriage is ending. Bob has clearly lost touch with reality.

There are so many examples that I could give to you, to try to convince you of his desperate need for help, but that seems redundant. Simply said—he needs help, and, therefore, my mother needs help as well.

So, I ask you to push Bob to explore his feelings. He seems to look forward to his time with you, but it almost seems like he sees his time with you as social hour.

*        *        *        *

**Marie:** *Over the next six weeks, the psychiatrist prescribed a number of medications, but Bob grew steadily worse. Finally the psychiatrist decided to refer Bob to a neurologist to explore organic causes.*

*In August 2003, we met with the Neurologist, Dr. Ronny Antelo. He thoroughly examined Bob and collected background information from me. He ordered an ultrasound, an MRI, and*

*an EEG. When we returned in October, Dr. Antelo said that the
EEG showed inconsistencies in Bob's brain and that the MRI
showed brain shrinkage. He told us that we might be looking
at dementia, but given Bob's relatively young age, he wanted to
run some more tests. Dr. Antelo ordered a spinal tap,
neuropsych testing, and blood work.*

*On December 18, 2003, my husband, Bob, was diagnosed with
Frontotemporal Dementia. He was 47 years old.*

*My initial thoughts were, 'Thank God, it has a name.' While
my mind told me that Bob's behavior, the source of so much
pain, was not his fault, it was still difficult to accept that Bob
could no longer control his impulses.*

A medical evaluation, leading to a diagnosis, provides some real
benefits. Some families learn, for example, that their loved one's
impairments are related to a treatable medical condition (severe
depression, for example), and with this knowledge in hand, they can
move quickly to resolve or relieve the problems.

For many families, however, evaluation confirms a suspicion. The
loved one has been stricken by a progressive, dementing illness that is
steadily eroding cognitive skills and slowly undermining basic
abilities.

This shocking, painful, and disturbing information can evoke the
family's deepest fears, but it can also prove helpful. It can provide
reassuring knowledge that baffling behavior is related to a specific
medical condition that can be understood and addressed. It can help
family members move from ambiguity to certainty, from ambivalence
and indecision to action and planning for the future. It can also help
the family envision a future that includes the Frontotemporal Dementia
reality.

Diagnosis helps the family in another critical way. It allows them to fully acknowledge the reality of the illness and to bring it into family life. Recognition and acceptance of the disease, through intellectual and emotional processing of the diagnosis, helps families achieve a new identity. The afflicted family member is now a patient with an identifiable disease, and the family members must move into a caregiving phase.

# CHAPTER FIVE

# FAMILY CAREGIVING

The caregiving phase is marked by an inescapable reality: a treasured loved one is losing the ability to carry out independent, adult activities. Family members must now find ways to meet emerging care challenges, while maintaining family stability and well-being.

As cognitive abilities decline, the afflicted family member becomes a care *receiver*, and family members become *caregivers*. The family has acclimated to the decline of their loved one through the prediagnosis and diagnosis phases. They must now, in the early caregiving phase, reorganize in ways that foster new relationships and address mounting care challenges.

## Frontotemporal Dementia embarks on two journeys:

- The afflicted individual's biological, emotional, psychological, and spiritual journey.

- The family's psychosocial journey (its experience with the illness).

Each journey poses special challenges and complexities that defy a "one size fits all" approach. When we see the family experience in terms of two journeys, we see more clearly the ways in which Frontotemporal Dementia evolves into a "family illness." We see the need for an adaptive, learning family system that continually accommodates and reacts to shifting realities and care challenges.

Frontotemporal Dementia strikes at family life through the cognitive and personality impairments it creates in its victims. These losses rob afflicted individuals not only of hard won skills, but also of the qualities that have made them unique. Over time, the FTD individual begins to seem *there* but *not there*. The patient is physically present but increasingly psychologically and emotionally absent.

Increasingly, the unpredictable behavior begins to affect family relationships. The illness, an uninvited, unwelcome intruder, begins to insidiously and relentlessly invade all domains of family life. It takes up residence. It begins to dominate family routines and rituals. For many families, the disease becomes a "family illness," an enveloping, pervasive, inescapable presence that casts a dark shadow over all family activities.

> **Marie**: *It was difficult to understand and accept why Bob, on some days, could perform certain activities, and then on other days would seem to lose the ability to think clearly. He was easily distracted. He became self-centered, which was highly uncharacteristic. In the presence of family, friends, and medical professionals, however, he could compensate for his symptoms, and he could control his impulses. One day on our way to an appointment with the neurologist, Bob said, 'I'm going to tell Dr. Antelo I don't have that dementia thing.' I think he expected me to object, but I didn't react. I said,*

*'That's fine,' understanding that Dr. Antelo would know the best way to handle this remark.*

*Dr. Antelo entered the exam room; greeted us and asked Bob how he was doing. Bob quickly responded with 'I don't have that dementia thing.' Dr. Antelo spoke with Bob about the recent changes in his behavior. He then, gently and diplomatically explained to Bob that he had many years of experience as a doctor and felt confident in his diagnosis. Dr. Antelo seemed to have addressed Bob's concern.*

*Frontotemporal Dementia is often misdiagnosed, but Dr. Antelo quickly diagnosed Bob. He was genuinely concerned about Bob, Michelle and me. He was supportive and very patient. He was always available to speak with me whenever I had a question or concern. One Sunday, when Bob was having a bad reaction to a new medication, I called Dr. Antelo to express my concern. I began to apologize for bothering him on a Sunday, when he said, 'You're not bothering me. Taking care of my patients is what I do. You can call me anytime.' I greatly admire Dr. Antelo as a physician and as a person. He was truly one of our many blessings.*

*As Bob entered each new phase in his illness, Dr. Antelo would begin to prepare me for what was next to come. He advised me on what to expect for Bob, the disease, and what measures I would have to take to keep him safe. The 'stepping in' actions were difficult. I had to take the car keys from Bob and confiscate his credit card. Things that drove me crazy, however, became funny when I'd relate them to Michelle. That's not to say we were laughing at Bob, but we had to learn to laugh a little. Here's an example. Bob forgot to tell me that he'd run out of his Zocor medication (for cholesterol). When I asked him about his need for the medication, he said that it was OK to miss a few days because he was eating Cheerios for breakfast. Cheerios commercials had started to claim that the cereal might help lower cholesterol. So, in Bob's mind the problem was covered. Following this incident, I began to monitor his medications more closely.*

*Over time, Michelle and I found ourselves transitioning from being wife and daughter to being parent and caregiver. Our hearts would break repeatedly with each new phase of the disease and its set of symptoms. The term "heartache" had taken on an entirely new meaning. The disease was progressive, and we knew each day that this was as good as it would ever be for Bob.*

*During this time, Bob's unemployment benefits had run out, and the financial pressures were growing. I was worried sick. I work in the Information Services Department of a life insurance company. One day, while speaking with a coworker, Janine, I told her about Bob's illness. In the course of our conversation, Janine asked me if Bob had applied for Long-Term Disability and Waiver of Premium on his life insurance. I told her that when I'd contacted the Human Resources department of Bob's former employer to inform them of his diagnosis, I asked if he was eligible for any disability benefits. I was told that Bob was not eligible, since the diagnosis was made after his termination on July 1, 2003.*

*Janine felt that Bob was eligible for Long-Term Disability and Waiver of Premium, due to the nature of his illness and the fact that onset occurred while he was still employed. The illness explained his poor job performance. Janine referred me to Dick, the Director of our company's Disability Department, who was an answer to my prayers.*

*When Dick and I met, I described Bob's diagnosis and the reasons for his job termination. Dick said, 'Absolutely, Bob is eligible for these benefits.' Bob was eventually approved for both of these benefits by his former employer. I soon developed a new friendship and a great source of support.*

*Michelle*: *One afternoon, I received a phone call from my parents' neighbor, Kathy. A friend of hers, who lives about a quarter mile down the road from them, had seen Bob walking along the highway near her home. Kathy told me that her husband, Kevin, was on his way to try to find Bob. I went to assist, but could not locate Bob or Kevin.*

*Kathy called back to let me know that Kevin had found Bob in the parking lot of Village Cuts and that he was safe. I remembered my mom had an appointment to have her hair cut there after work. I knew that I had to try and make Bob understand the danger of walking that far by himself. When I pulled into the parking lot to pick him up, I tried to put my "angry" face on, but Bob was so happy to see me that nothing else mattered to him. He was in his glory. He assumed I was there to surprise my mom, too. As an added bonus, to his delight, Kevin and I had both shown up! He was very happy.*

*When I think about it now, it seems sweet that Bob wanted to surprise my mom. It was, however, incredibly dangerous. They lived near a busy road with dangerous traffic patterns and, in some parts, little room for pedestrians. While Bob's retrieval was going on, my mom was on the train returning home from work.*

*I explained to Bob that he was endangering himself. He replied that he hadn't walked the entire way, that a "friend" had given him a ride. I said, 'I know that Kevin didn't give you a ride.' Bob said, 'No, not Kevin.' I almost let that go, but then I asked, 'Who gave you a ride?' Bob said, 'My friend.' I asked, 'What friend?' Bob said, 'I don't know. He just gave me a ride.' Imagine my panic. Like a child, Bob had accepted a ride from a total stranger. Thankfully, the driver was kind enough to drive Bob to his intended destination safely and did not take advantage of his childlike innocence. Although Bob was proud of his accomplishment, it was an obvious display to my mom and I that his judgment had declined significantly.*

**Marie**: *Bob became increasingly self-centered; it was so unlike him. Birthdays became important to Bob. Two weeks before his forty-ninth birthday, he called his siblings to remind them of his upcoming birthday. He asked each sibling if he or she would be sending a card. The "Old Bob" would never have been so bold!*

*A strong appetite for sweets is often a symptom of FTD. Due to a cardiac condition, Bob had been restricted from caffeine and stimulants such as chocolate for several years. I came home from work one day to find wrappers from half of a bag of Hershey Kisses in the kitchen trash container. I became alarmed and told Bob that he couldn't have that much chocolate again. So, he resourcefully began flushing the wrappers down the toilet. He gained skill in compensating for the disease, a common response.*

*Bob also became extremely time conscious—down to the minute. He engaged in repetitive behaviors. The expression "broken record syndrome" took on an entirely new meaning. Bob was unable to resist his impulses and it became progressively more difficult to redirect him. He became a fast eater; he began to "inhale" his food. He couldn't sit for any length of time; he seemed restless and always on the move.*

*Bob would blast his music like a teenager, especially his favorite – the Hawaii Five-O theme song. He had others that he played over and over again at high volume, all the while beaming and laughing. At times, our next-door neighbors could hear Bob's music in their house, during the winter, with the windows closed.*

*I ordered a Safe Return bracelet for Bob and caregiver's bracelets for Michelle and me from the Alzheimer's Association. I asked Michelle to give them to us as gifts, because I knew how much Bob loved her and would want to please her. At the right moment, she put the bracelet on his wrist and said, 'I have one for my mom, too.' She showed Bob that she, too, was wearing a Safe Return bracelet. At first, Bob would repeatedly take the bracelet off and then put it back on. One weekend, Bob's parents took him for the weekend to give me some respite time. They picked Bob up before I returned home from work. When I went to our room, to change from my work clothes, I noticed Bob's bracelet sitting on the nightstand. My immediate thought was, if he wanders away from his parents' home anytime this weekend, the bracelet is sitting uselessly on the nightstand instead of on his wrist! Again we were blessed, as Bob's visit with his parent's resulted in his safe return home on Sunday.*

*Eventually he wore the bracelet all the time. He would frequently look at it and say, 'This says Safe Return.' Michelle and I would reply, 'So does mine,' He would say, 'It does?'*

\*   \*   \*   \*

*In September 2004, our neighbor, Kathy, made Michelle aware of some problems that were occurring while I was at work.*

*Bob would go out to the bus stop at the bottom of our driveway everyday and became too comfortable with the neighbors. He had been following them home and talking along the way. Bob tried to enter one of the neighbor's homes without knocking and walked into another house twice without knocking.*

*Bob routinely went to the afternoon kindergarten bus stop and he picked children up in the air while saying 'Whee!' The children didn't like this, and neither did the parents.*

*One day, a thirteen-year-old girl went to the bus stop in the afternoon to pick up her sibling, and Bob tickled her, which upset her very much! One of the parents tried to explain Bob's illness to her, but that didn't console her. Kathy's mother was also at the bus stop that day, and when she told Bob to stop tickling the girl, he started tickling her.*

*He also approached the middle school age kids when they were walking home and tried to show them pictures of our trips.*

All these changes in behavior create increasing and unrelenting strain within the family system. The FTD patient's behavior is changing, often in disturbing ways. Family members see a loved one who, in some sense, seems familiar but who, in another sense, is beginning to seem like a total stranger.

The steady decline and changing behavior evokes feelings of grief and sadness and other forms of emotional pain for the family. The distress surrounding these changes can cause family members to step back and begin distancing themselves from the afflicted individual as well as from one another.

Dementia care creates special challenges for some understandable reasons.

- First, this kind of caregiving is an open-ended experience. It's difficult to know when one has done well. Thus, caregivers live in a constant state of uncertainty. In addition, without a clear sense of achievement, they find it difficult to maintain a sense of optimism about their care activities.

- Second, as the relationship with the loved one continues to change, caregivers begin to lose a sense of give and take in the relationship. They lose a sense that their efforts are understood and appreciated. The relationship becomes increasingly one-sided. Many caregivers ultimately find that they have little left to give.

- Third, caregivers can begin to feel isolated. Their lives may begin to revolve around caregiving. Interests and usual activities diminish. Enjoyment declines, and caregivers eventually find themselves deprived of any effective renewal and replenishment sources.

At some point in the caregiving phase, many families see evidence that care demands are damaging relationships and undermining family life. Families often reach the conclusion that "we can no longer go it alone and need some kind of outside help." Many families initially choose the adult day care option.

# CHAPTER SIX

## SHARED CARE

*F*amily resources vary, and each family will make a determination about outside care in its own way, based on its own assessment of the family's wants and needs. The decision to seek outside help in and of itself, however, signals the beginning of a major family system adaptation. It is the beginning or intensification of interactions with the health care system, which will continue through the rest of the illness.

The decision to seek help raises some basic questions.

- What kinds of assistance will help?
- What resources are available?
- How do we integrate outside help with the family caregiving system?
- How do we pay for care?
- What kind of help does the individual need?
- What assistance will benefit the caregivers?
- Who can advise us?

In the face of increasing care duties, some families still prefer to "go it alone," drawing only on family resources. Others choose to seek only the help of friends and other forms of informal support (self-help groups, for example). Many others, however, see a need to reach out for professional help and support. Unfortunately, many families see only one choice of outside help—placement in a long-term care facility. Many families, repelled by the idea of nursing home care, delay their decision to seek *any* kind of assistance.

In fact, outside help includes a continuum of services and programs, both formal and informal, which stretch between family care and nursing home care. With planning and advice, many families are able to knit together an effective set of community programs and services. Many turn to adult day care services.

*Marie*: *Bob started attending the Adult Day Program at Chandler Hall in November 2004. The facility had a good reputation and offered an affordable transportation program. Bob initially attended the program three days a week. I later increased his time to four days a week. On the fifth day, Bob's parents spent a couple of hours with him.*

*When still able to drive, Bob had occasionally performed volunteer work at a local hospital. When I told him I thought he would benefit from going to Chandler Hall, he seemed confused. He thought he might be working at the facility. He just wasn't sure what was going on. I explained that he wouldn't be working there, but that it would be good for him to be with other people, and to get out of the house during the day.*

*Bob's relatively young age and high level of mobility challenged the staff's capabilities. He was the youngest person in the program by far. In fact, he would occasionally point out that the people around him were old. Due to his age and mobility, the staff allowed him to visit the lobby area, just outside the day care room, and chat with the security guard. He also liked to sit in a chair and look out the window, observing the traffic and eyeing visitors to the multi-purpose building.*

*The building also housed a childcare program and a YMCA. Children would visit the adults a few times a week to spend some intergenerational time. One day, a little boy brought a storybook along and asked Bob to read to him. Bob happily complied. Some days he was unable to focus on reading, but when he could read, the children would gather around. A staff member took a picture of Bob with the children and posted it on the bulletin board. Bob was so proud of that picture. He removed it from the bulletin board, and brought it home, and proudly placed it on the refrigerator door. When Michelle and I were preparing to move Bob into an assisted living facility, we created a photo album for him, which included this picture.*

Bob reading to some children at Chandler Hall

*Bob, a curious person by nature, liked to explore, and he would often wander into the YMCA. When Bob wandered into the "Y," the director would call the day care staff and announce his presence. Someone from the staff would then return him to the day care area. Eventually, Bob began to follow people out of the building and accompany them to their cars—he wanted to converse. At that time, he was almost obsessed about describing a cruise that we'd taken to Bermuda. Our ship happened to be the Pacific Princess, the ship used on the television show Love Boat. Bob would explain over and over that he'd been on the actual Love Boat.*

*Chandler Hall's bus would pick Bob up about 9:00 a.m. and drop him off at home about 3:00 p.m. The adult day care services temporarily relieved my concerns about his safety. Since I did not return home from work, however, until about 5:30 p.m., this still left Bob by himself for nearly two-and-a-half hours.*

*Bob would anticipate my arrival and he'd often wait outside for me. We lived two houses from a very busy highway, and Bob had been spotted a few times walking on the highway. Neighbors would encourage Bob to return home, but he would often be back on the highway within minutes. Sometimes he would walk the curb like he was walking a tightrope.*

Bob waiting for my return home from work

One evening at dinner, I asked Bob about his day at Chandler Hall. It was the dead of winter and very cold, and we'd been hit by a snowstorm the previous day. Bob said, 'The policeman told me the road is very slippery.' I asked, 'What policeman?' After Bob returned from Chandler Hall, he had apparently been out in the middle of the highway, near our house, attempting to spot my car, and a policeman had cautioned him.

At this point, Bob didn't understand cause and effect. When I would express concern for his safety, he would say something like, 'But, I didn't get hit by a car.' Bob wanted me to be at home with him; I was a security blanket. When I was at home, he would retreat to the living room or the bedroom to "rest up."

My mother succumbed to cancer eighteen days after Bob began attending the Adult Day Program. Due to Bob's inappropriate behavior and his inability to sit for more than a few minutes, I made the difficult decision to exclude him from the viewing and memorial service. One of our dear friends, Scott, offered to keep Bob occupied at an evening church youth group activity. While at church, Bob desperately tried to get people to give him a ride to the funeral home. He wanted to be there for me.

It was a difficult evening for me, since "Old Bob" would have been by my side and would have been my rock, but I knew I couldn't mourn my mother's death with Bob at the funeral home. He was becoming very childlike. I would have had to parent him, a task that would have been upsetting to me, and generally disruptive. This was a difficult decision, but one of many I found myself making at this point and all through the rest of the journey.

It's a tradition in our area for Santa Claus to ride around neighborhoods on a fire truck on Christmas Eve. Each year Santa stops in front of our neighbors' house and greets the *children who are attending their Christmas Eve open house. The sight of Santa, sitting on the approaching fire truck, excited Bob. He ran outside, raced across our lawn, and jumped in front of all the children. As Santa climbed down from the truck, Bob was the first to shake his hand. When he'd finished greeting Santa, I was able to redirect him back inside our house until it was time to leave for the church service.*

*We arrived at church early; I was a member of the hand bell choir and the group planned to rehearse before the service began. I told Bob to sit in his seat and stay with Michelle until I returned. The minute I was out of sight, Bob climbed over the next row of chairs and ran toward the organ. Michelle ran after him and physically pulled him away from the organ. He kept saying, 'I know how to play the organ.' Bob had grown up in churches, and he no doubt had played an organ at one time, but he wasn't known to be an organist, and his talents weren't especially needed that Christmas Eve when choirs were trying to rehearse. As a result of Bob's disruptive behavior, Michelle took Bob home.*

*At some point in the journey, I began to consciously focus attention on my blessings. This became a type of coping mechanism. I had much to be thankful for, and I made it a point to look for the positive things in my life. As the disease progressed, I felt blessed that Bob could still recognize me and could still express his love for me. I felt blessed that family members and friends cared so much about me and about Bob. I was thankful to be included in their prayers.*

*Nevertheless, I struggled at times with depression. Some days the world seemed very dark and forbidding. The phrase "broken heart" took on deeper meanings. The progressive nature of the disease was gut wrenching. Each loss forced a change in my relationship with Bob. There was no stopping the losses and no stopping the increasing loss of a "husband."*

*This once vibrant, intelligent man was becoming a child encased in an adult's body.*

*I shed tears, but I kept going. I don't how I kept going at times, but my faith in God continued to grow. I knew that it was by the grace of God I was able to keep my full-time job, my part-time job, and, indeed, my sanity. My body at times seemed to be on auto-pilot. I don't know how I did what I did. I just did it.*

*I lived each day knowing that this was as good as it would ever get. I yearned for the status quo. When people asked how I was doing, I initially responded with the phrase "peaks and valleys." As time went on, I began to reply, "plateaus and valleys."*

*Bob continued to see his Neurologist, Dr. Antelo, who would tell me that the disease was progressing rapidly. I didn't ask about life expectancy. What was the point? I knew I would give Bob everything I could, for as long as I could.*

Even when outside care needs are obvious, some families find it difficult to ask for help, and too many families wait too long. They wait for a crisis, and then they find themselves making decisions and establishing relationships in an emergency. In a crisis, there is no time to fully evaluate or develop effective relationships with outside forms of support.

Early planning and identification of suitable services can ease the transition into shared care. Smooth interactions between family caregivers and outside help can pave the way for a partnership that joins unique skills and knowledge that help both professionals and family members reach their goals.

For many families, however, care demands eventually begin to outstrip both family *and* supportive outside care resources, including day care programs. Many families eventually turn to a long-term care option.

# CHAPTER SEVEN

# ASSISTED LIVING - MILL RUN

*T*he long-term care phase is marked by the recognition that home care and programs such as adult day care are reaching their limits. Not all families will choose long-term care, but most families, at some point, will consider such care.

It's difficult to define the precise moment at which a family should begin thinking about long-term care. Some families reach the decision when an "expert" (usually a physician or perhaps, an informed family member) tells them that the "time is now." Other families make the decision when the patient's behavior and health problems simply exceed family caregiving and various supportive capabilities.

*Marie*: *In the beginning of the New Year, Michelle and I began to plan for the next step in Bob's care. Bob's time at the Adult Day Program at Chandler Hall allowed us time to search for a long-term care facility. We were looking ahead, anticipating placement needs.*

*The search proved frustrating for several reasons. First, people didn't understand that I needed not only a suitable place for Bob, but also one I could afford. Assisted Living costs are not covered by health insurance. I worried about how I would support two households, his and mine. Moreover, the search itself became a dreadful task, laden with painful feelings. Some of the facilities seemed cold and clinical. Others simply wouldn't consider Bob. They thought he was too mobile, and they did not wish to deal with a potential runaway. Michelle and I agreed that a suitable facility had to feel right.*

*One day, while Michelle and I were running errands, we passed by a facility called Sunrise at Floral Vale. We stopped by and met with Christine, the Director of Community Relations, who gave us a tour. The facility seemed just right, but I felt it was unaffordable. Christine then referred us to another less costly Sunrise facility, Mill Run, ten miles away. We met with Sandy, the Director of Community Relations, and described the care challenges that go with Frontotemporal Dementia. We then made an appointment to meet with Chris, the facility's nurse, to evaluate Bob.*

*We met the next week, and fortunately, Bob was compensating very well that day. He was able to sit through a forty-five minute meeting, and he answered all of Chris' questions in an appropriate fashion.*

*Chris told us that they could accept Bob, but that he would have to wear a Wander Guard bracelet to alert them when he was approaching the front door. She said that Bob would have his own room, and, as the disease progressed, he would eventually move to their locked dementia floor. The environment seemed just right, and we made the decision to move Bob, a decision made out of love and deep concern for his safety.*

*I knew we had made the right decision to move Bob into a facility where he would be monitored, but it broke my heart. I knew it was a major turning point, and the decision caused me to reflect even more deeply on my experience with the illness up to this point. How had I coped? How had I faced such a harsh reality? What were my feelings about Bob and about the ugly disease?*

*After making the decision to place Bob in this facility, Michelle and I worked to prepare Bob's room. Without his knowledge, we stocked it with familiar objects: photos of the three of us, his college diploma, Goofy and Star Trek memorabilia, a watercolor painting of a scene in Bermuda painted by Bob's mother.*

**Michelle**: *I knew my mother was agonizing over how and what to tell Bob about the move. I offered to help with the announcement, to provide moral support. The actual event was truly heartbreaking. The thought that Bob would never see his home again depressed me, and I can't imagine what was going through his mind. He kept saying to my mom, 'I'm not interested in a room at Mill Run. I want to sleep in bed next to you at night.'*

\*    \*    \*    \*    \*

**Marie**: *Bob was frightened and confused. His world was about to change in ways that he couldn't comprehend. On Wednesday, May 18, 2005, Bob moved into the Mill Run Assisted Living Facility.*

*Mill Run's policy does not allow new residents to have visitors for the first few days. I was concerned about this policy, since I knew Bob's new surroundings would be confusing to him. Staff members asked me to trust them and to let them do their job in helping Bob adjust to his new home.*

*The first day was difficult for everyone—Bob, Michelle, me, and all the folks at Mill Run. Bob was determined to return home and he ran from the building several times. I received a number of phone calls from Chris, the nurse who had initially assessed Bob, and she was frantic. Bob's behavior was frightening to the staff because they were not prepared for a young, strong, mobile man like Bob! They surrounded Bob to try to prevent him from going toward the door, and he broke through the circle. This behavior came as a surprise to the staff because they were unfamiliar with FTD and had not researched it. At Bob's evaluation, he compensated for the disease so well, that although I described Bob's typical behavior, they had not seen what I expressed.*

*During one phone call that first day, Chris insisted I take Bob to a hospital and have his medications adjusted. On another call, she asked me to have Bob's neurologist and psychiatrist adjust the medications in order to calm him. She also asked me to call Friend's Hospital in Philadelphia to arrange for admission. When that didn't work out, she told me I needed to admit Bob to the Mental Health Unit at Lower Bucks Hospital. She was extremely anxious, which was very upsetting and frustrating to me.*

*Michelle and our friend, Denice were with me while I was receiving the calls. Denice suggested that she and Michelle take Bob to Lower Bucks Hospital. She thought my presence might upset Bob, and I think she correctly concluded that Bob could not tolerate another separation from me.*

*Denice is a Pediatrician on staff at Lower Bucks Hospital. When she called the Emergency Room to inquire about having Bob admitted, she was told that the hospital could not accept Bob into their Mental Health Unit due to the Pennsylvania Mental Health Procedures Act of 1976. This Act does not allow patients to be treated without consent unless they are posing a danger to themselves or others. Bob was not capable of making the decision to be admitted. After some tense conversations with Chris at Mill Run and phone calls to Bob's neurologist, we were able to get his medications adjusted. Bob eventually settled down for the night without incident, partly due to sheer exhaustion.*

*Bob's initial adjustment period took longer than expected. So we were told to wait a few more days before visiting. We waited a week, which must have seemed like an eternity to Bob.*

*Fortunately, Bob was resourceful. On his first day at Mill Run, he had located a telephone in the Bistro (main lobby) that was available for general use—and so, the phone calls began. It was wonderful to hear his voice, but so sad to hear his despair.*

*Michelle and I went together for the first visit. We were very apprehensive about how Bob would respond, and we wondered if he would attempt to leave with us. He was ecstatic to see us!*

*Bob showed us around the facility, and then we went into the courtyard for a short visit. We stayed there just long enough to eat the water ice that we had brought as a treat. Then he took us to his room.*

*We entered his room, and he lay down on his bed. He asked me to lie down beside him, which was a challenge. Two adults in one twin bed did not work well. This was the beginning of the way in which Bob and I would spend time on future visits.*

## An Evolution of Love

*Bob would often tell me that he wanted to sleep in bed next to me at night. To hear him say this broke my heart. I missed him so much, but I knew he couldn't be home alone any longer.*

*Bob and Michelle spent many visits watching television. When Bob watched television, he would turn up the volume and blare the theme songs from Action News, Pennsylvania Lottery, etc. He would laugh when he did this. He thought it was funny. When it was close to the time for my arrival, they would spend the remaining time walking around the parking lot.*

*As Bob settled in at Mill Run, our relationship began to change—it improved. The repetition, the annoying and frustrating behaviors, began to seem cute. We were able to spend quality time together, which was good for all three of us.*

*Bob could be loving, funny and challenging, all at the same time. He became very methodical and his entire day revolved around time. Breakfast was at 8:00 a.m., then he would call to ask, 'What time are you coming?' He would sit in a chair outside the general store until it opened at 10:00 a.m., when he would buy a bag of Skittles candy. Sometime before lunch he would call me again to ask, 'What time are you coming?'*

*Next was lunch and then a few more phone calls to ask, 'What time are you coming?' Finally, dinner was at 5:00 p.m. and then off to the Bistro in the main lobby, to wait for me. Unfortunately, this was a difficult time for Bob and the staff. He could not control his impulse to go outside and wait for me. Most evenings when I arrived, I would find a few employees in the Bistro with Bob, trying to prevent him from running out the front door to greet me. As time went on, and when staffing permitted, employees found it easier to take Bob outside and walk him around the parking lot until I arrived.*

*Michelle and I had long been immersing ourselves in our new roles of caregiver and parent, but now we reached a new level. Looking back, I realize that this is the time we'd finally accepted the behaviors associated with the disease. We were truly beginning to know "New Bob" at another level, and our love grew even stronger. Our visits with Bob were very special. He always trusted me, and that trust continued throughout the journey.*

Michelle, Bob and Marie at Mill Run on Father's Day 2005

*Bob finally adjusted to the routines at Mill Run, but he continued to challenge their care capabilities. He was mindful of time and was a "runner." He would bolt out the door at the first opportunity. Bob wanted to go outside, and do his own thing. After all, that's what he'd been doing all his life.*

*Most of my visits began with a series of staff complaints about Bob's behavior. In the beginning, I tried to reason with him. Of course, that didn't work, given the nature of the disease.*

*The facility had a spacious courtyard, but Bob didn't care to spend time there because he didn't like the fence. The staff always told Bob what he couldn't do, but they did not attempt to redirect him.*

*As his attempts to get outside persisted, the Mill Run management began to have second thoughts about Bob's continued residence. They told me they didn't have the staffing to provide individual attention to Bob. Their solution was for me to hire a companion for four hours a day to help out. I viewed this as a "baby sitting" request, and I felt that it was unreasonable, since I was paying them to provide care. I also knew that four hours a day wouldn't satisfy their need as Bob was a challenge for them throughout the entire day. Essentially, they were asking me to hire someone to sit and be available to walk with Bob when he wanted to go outside. After a meeting with the director of the facility and a support staff member, I was given two weeks to come up with a plan.*

**Michelle:** *I called the director to discuss a matter and was put through to the staff support person who had attended the meeting with my mother. In the course of the conversation, the staff member commented to me that they'd asked my mom to get back to them with her plan, and they'd not heard from her yet. I was quick to point out that it hadn't been two weeks since the meeting. Then the support person made an admission; if we didn't agree to supply a paid companion, the facility would give us thirty days to relocate Bob.*

**Marie:** *After making some phone calls to get information about hiring a companion, I learned that the added cost associated with this request in addition to what I was already paying Mill Run was comparable to having Bob at a specialized facility, such as Floral Vale.*

Assisted Living facilities are designed to meet the needs of the elderly with varying needs by providing meals, assisting with personal needs, and the distribution of medication. Many facilities have dementia units; however, few specialize in dementia like Sunrise at Floral Vale. All the residents in Floral Vale's home have some type of dementia, which makes their facility unique. Also, it is a small facility which enables the staff to get to know all of the residents on a personal level.

Caregivers working with people with Frontotemporal Dementia need training in understanding the difference between FTD and other dementias such as Alzheimer's. The symptoms of FTD are more behavioral than memory related, which presents a different type of challenge. Also, FTD often occurs when people are in their 40's or 50's and are physically stronger than an older person.

Relying on professional care can pose challenges to an FTD patient's family. Having dealt with the illness since its onset, family members have a better understanding of how to best handle many situations, even when the patient is residing in a home such as Floral Vale. Where family members may be a part of the care team for patients with other types of illness, the family very much acts as the team leader in the case of FTD.

*Marie: Frontotemporal Dementia is rare and Bob was the first resident with this form of dementia at both Mill Run and later at Floral Vale. The staff continually learned as the disease progressed, but Michelle and I had a running start, and ultimately, knew the core of who Bob was and how he would best fare in many situations better than the professionals.*

# CHAPTER EIGHT

# ASSISTED LIVING - FLORAL VALE

Eventually, Bob transferred to another assisted living facility, Sunrise at Floral Vale.

**Marie:** *We moved Bob to Floral Vale on August 1, 2005, and he appeared to be at ease almost immediately. Bob began introducing himself to the other residents, which was unusual behavior for him. He took on the role of greeter and introduced himself to everyone who entered the building. As a result, other resident's family members, doctors, physical therapists, and vendors all knew Bob! He touched many lives, even during his illness, and they all developed fond feelings toward him.*

*Bob's days continued to revolve around time. He would repeatedly say, 'I'm going to call my wife at 10:00; I'm going to call my wife at 2:00; my wife is coming at 6:30.' Although he knew my normal arrival time, he would still always ask me what time I was coming. I think he needed the reassurance. He would look at his digital watch and observe the minutes changing, while informing everyone around of the current time. Try listening to that over a period of time!*

*The Director of Community Relations at Floral Vale, Rita, suggested I send occasional emails to Bob at her address, as an additional means of communicating during the day. Bob replied to my emails from Rita's office. Rita said he still knew his way around a computer. She was often able to redirect Bob by telling him she needed help with her computer.*

*During the time that the phone was still important to Bob, he would often find an empty office and call me. He was still able to dial the phone on his own.*

*Bob liked having his independence. He had a key to the door of my car, and he liked to unlock the door before sitting in the passenger seat. Bob also continued to carry his wallet, which contained his pictures and insurance cards. He liked to make his own decisions. Whenever possible, we would give Bob two options. This would allow him to make a choice.*

**Michelle:** *Bob liked to take car rides with my mom and me. We usually had no destination in mind, so we would ask Bob for directions, and he would guide us. We frequently went to the food court at the mall for pizza. He would often ask me to take him home. He would say things like, 'It would just be so much easier if you would take me home, so I could sleep next to your mom.' He would then give me their street address, the name of their development, and town.*

*I would respond with, 'I'll get in trouble if I don't take you back, because I signed you out.' Bob would try to assure me that I wouldn't get into trouble, but then he'd eventually agree to return to Floral Vale. Sometimes when Bob and I were by ourselves and my mom was due to visit, I would say, 'My mom won't know where to find you if I don't take you back.' This always worked.*

**Marie:** *Floral Vale employed a maintenance man by the name of Bob. Periodically, the staff would summon him by loudspeaker. They would announce, 'Bob, please come to the front desk.' Our Bob would promptly arrive, and then the concierge would give him something or find something for him to do, just to make his trip worthwhile.*

*The Floral Vale facility is divided into two neighborhoods. Inside the door of each neighborhood is a photo album showing the name of each resident and his or her care manager. Bob liked to look through this album, and when he'd see the phrase Care Manager next to his photo, he would assume that he, indeed, was one of the care managers. After all, they'd been paging him several times a week. We jokingly asked Betty, the director, if Bob's status as "Care Manager" entitled us to an "employee discount." She laughed and turned us down. No such luck.*

*Food was a priority in Bob's day, and this lasted all the way up to the last month or so of his illness. In fact, I tell people that he had two priorities—food and me. I think in that order! He would sit in the dining room waiting for his meals. He would sometimes sit for an hour or more, which was amazing because he usually couldn't sit in one spot more than five or ten minutes.*

*The other important priority in Bob's life was spending time with me. He made two phone calls to me each day and the first thing he asked was, 'What time are you coming tonight?' He would then proceed to tell everyone he came in contact with,*

*'My wife is coming at 6:30.' He repeated that statement over and over again. I drove a white car at the time and whenever Bob saw a white car in the parking lot, he would attempt to flee the building. He thought I was arriving, even though I'd just spoken to him minutes before. One day when Bob was trying to go out the front door, a staff member asked him what he would do if he couldn't find his way back to Floral Vale. He pointed to his Safe Return bracelet and said, 'That's why I have this.' His attempts to get outside were relentless. He had moves. Like a good football running back, he would dart in one direction, and then shift directions, pulling the staff member out of position.*

*The staff was usually successful in blocking Bob from the door, but there were other times when the coast was clear and he was able to make a quick escape. From what the staff at Floral Vale told me, Bob was typically cooperative in returning to the building; however, he was resourceful too. When he saw visitors enter the building, he would try to make a run for it. People who did not know that Bob lived at Floral Vale, were accommodating in holding the door open for him to exit the building. With his young age, they had no reason to think that Bob was a resident and Bob took full advantage of those opportunities.*

*My visits almost always included some time lying in bed next to Bob. In the winter, I would often rub my cold hands on his and tell him how warm his hands felt. One night, while simply resting my hand on his, he said, 'Your hand isn't moving.' I smiled and said, 'You're right. Thank you for reminding me.'*

*He would often adjust my engagement and wedding rings, so that they lined up straight on my finger. He would also show me his bracelet and point out the words "Safe Return." I would tell him that Michelle's bracelet and mine said the same thing. Then he would smile. His loving and nurturing nature would again show, and I cherished those special moments.*

*During the ten months Bob spent in the Assisted Living facilities, I visited him often. I would occasionally be asked why I made such frequent visits. My answer was always the same: 'Why not? He is my husband, and I love him.' Bob loved those visits and I cherished our time together. I also believed that there would come a time when Bob would no longer recognize me. So these times were truly special.*

*When Bob was well, we had always enjoyed going out to dinner. As the disease progressed, the restaurant staff and other customers began to notice Bob's unusual behavior. I began carrying business-sized cards that said, 'Please excuse my husband's behavior. He has dementia. Thank you for your patience.' I would leave them on the table when we left the restaurant. This was a way of communicating to the server that Bob had an illness—a disease that caused him to behave differently. It also saved me from having to make explanations. I used them only a few times, but they were a source of comfort.*

*Eventually Michelle and I found it easier to eat at the Food Court at the mall, where Bob could just get up and walk around. He liked pizza, and he liked to order his own slice. Bob would often state that he didn't have any money and he would ask Michelle or me if we could pay. We would assure him that we could, and then he would smile from ear to ear. Bob liked to make the payment himself. He would take the money from our hand and give it to the cashier. Then he would give the change back to us.*

*After pizza, Bob would often ask me if I wanted to do some shopping. When healthy, Bob had been a great shopping partner, but now his attention span had shortened and I was unable to shop with him. One time, when the Christmas decorations had gone up in the mall, Bob asked if I wanted to look for a sweater for Michelle. After that, we looked almost every week. He would choose a department store (he still remembered where each was located), and we'd look around. Bob would soon tire and we'd return to Floral Vale without making a purchase. He was satisfied that we shopped for a sweater for Michelle even though we did not make a purchase.*

*On one occasion at Floral Vale, his unacceptable behavior took a physical form. We removed him from the facility for a few days to have him evaluated for possible medication adjustment. The closest facility was the Frankford Hospital Behavioral Health Unit for Older Adults. In the past, they had refused to accept Bob because they considered him too young (one had to be 55 years or older). This was a frustrating matter for me. He seemed too young for programs that might have benefited him; however he didn't seem too young to contract the disease.*

*The psychiatrist who visited some of the residents at Floral Vale was on staff at Frankford Hospital Behavioral Health Unit for Older Adults. After she described Bob's illness to the Medical Director, Bob was admitted, and Michelle and I escorted him to Frankford-Bucks. Bob didn't want to stay there; he wanted to return to Floral Vale. He was frightened and didn't understand why he was there.*

*The next afternoon Michelle and I went to visit Bob. He was very restless and wanted me to take him home to Floral Vale. Staff members were able to let themselves out of the unit by using an electronic keypad, a security device. Bob spent time pressing the buttons. He was trying to break out.*

*Michelle and I left the hospital at 4:30 p.m. At approximately 6:00 p.m., I received a phone call from the Behavioral Unit nurse. She said, 'Bob is fine, but we had a little problem.' She explained that by randomly pressing the buttons on the keypad, Bob had somehow managed to hit the combination of keys that opened the door and he had left the Unit! The nurses alerted* security, who found him in the parking lot trying to open the doors of white cars, the cars that resembled my car. It was a chilly October evening, and so a security guard said to him, 'Bob, it's cold out here. Let's go back inside and get your jacket'. Bob agreed, and he returned calmly to the Unit. The staff had to close the escape entrance and cover the keypad to conceal it from Bob.

Bob was always a resourceful individual and this quality did not totally desert him in his illness period. He could cleverly find his way into parts of the facility that were off limits. He could get through a seeming maze of doors—always a surprise to the staff at Floral Vale.

Bob also retained his nurturing qualities. He looked after other residents almost like a big brother. He seemed especially protective of his roommate, Nick. If he heard someone coughing, he would hand them a cup of water. On occasion, Bob would push Theresa, a wheelchair bound resident, to the dining room and to Town Square. He would remind Donald, with whom he shared a mealtime table, when it was time to eat. When Michelle broke her ankle, Bob found it unsettling to see her in a cast and on crutches.

Bob continued to take pride in his appearance throughout the disease. When he had been lying in bed, as he often did, and was about to leave his room, he would always brush his hair. He chose his clothes each day and dressed appropriately, until the last month or two of his life. It was winter and Bob always wore a short-sleeved golf shirt under his sweatshirt. Some days he would put the golf shirt on backwards. When the staff or I offered to help him adjust it, he would say, 'That's OK. I like it this way.' We would allow him to make that decision, and he would wear his shirt the way he wanted to wear it for the day.

*Bob loved to receive mail. Friends and family members showered him with cards. He saved every piece, and we displayed them at his funeral.*

*Bob's love for music continued at Floral Vale. There was a radio near the front desk that he'd listen to. If he liked the song that was playing, he would blast the volume. One day, the volume became a problem for Jen, who worked at the front desk. She was on the phone with a family member of a perspective resident, and she was trying to get Bob to turn down the volume so she could conduct her conversation. Bob smiled and said, 'Just have fun!' Jen had to climb under the desk in order to communicate with the prospective client. The staff finally curtailed Bob's adjusting of the volume by moving the radio behind the desk.*

**Michelle:** *In October 2005, my mom and I walked in the Alzheimer's Association Memory Walk. We formed our own team and called it "Team Bob Sykes." I made t-shirts with a picture of the three of us on them. When we went to visit Bob after the walk, he was thrilled to see our pictures on our shirts and his name above them.*

Memory Walk 2005

**Marie:** *Bob liked to be independent. When he was at Mill Run, he was able to have a few dollars in his wallet, so that he could buy his daily bag of Skittles candy from the snack shop. At Floral Vale, however, we weren't able to leave money in his wallet because it would "disappear." With Christmas season approaching, the lack of money became an issue for Bob. He wanted to buy a gift for me, but said he couldn't because he didn't have any money.*

*Michelle had offered to help Bob pick out a gift for me, but she had recently broken her ankle and was on crutches, and I felt that it would be difficult for her to accompany him. In the event he wouldn't cooperate with Michelle, she would be unable to run after him.*

*As luck would have it, we had a snowstorm one day in early December. Michelle and I were both home from work that day. The sun came out in the afternoon, and the snow began to melt. Michelle and I decided to visit Bob that afternoon. We thought this might be a good time for him to do his Christmas shopping. Michelle and I first went to a nearby Hallmark store to browse. I showed Michelle a few items I thought Bob might like to "choose" for me. Bob and I had always exchanged gifts, so he felt the need to have a gift for me.*

**Michelle:** *When we went to Floral Vale to pick Bob up, I pulled him aside and asked if he'd like to go Christmas shopping for my mom. Bob became so excited that his eyes filled up with tears. Once we got to the Hallmark store, my mom went off to look at other things while I shopped with Bob. I asked him if he would like to choose a card. Bob used to select beautiful cards for her and write a sentimental message in each. This day, I led him to the wife section, and he selected the largest card he could find. It was a beautiful card, but he hadn't even opened it. I asked Bob if that was the card he wanted, to which he responded, 'Yes, it is!'*

*Next, we discussed a gift selection for my mom. I made a few suggestions, and Bob chose a Lenox snowman. When we took the item to the cashier, Bob became confused, because the employee took the snowman from him to put back on the shelf. She simply wanted to give Bob a new snowman in a box, but Bob didn't understand. It seemed to him that we'd just bought a snowman, and now they wouldn't let him have it. Fortunately, my mom was able to redirect Bob by showing him something in the store while I completed the transaction with the sales associate.*

*I took the snowman home with me and promised Bob that I would pick him up on Friday after work and take him to my house so we could wrap the gift. We had decided that my mom would later bring a pizza and that the three of us would have dinner together. When I took Bob to my house that evening, he was more interested in watching TV and waiting outside for my mom's arrival than the gift wrapping. These are the kinds of things we learned to laugh about.*

**Marie:** *Bob took the Christmas card with him back to Floral Vale. A few nights later when I visited him, he was out in Town Square waiting for me. He had the signed card in his hand. He walked toward me, handed the card to me, and said, 'Here, this is for you.' I said, 'Honey, that is so sweet, but I don't have your card with me, so why don't we wait until another day.' With that he said, 'No, that's OK.' He took the card from my hand and proceeded to open it for me. I had to laugh, because he knew what he wanted, and he was going to get the job done. He handed the card back to me and proudly said, 'It's from me.' He was so pleased with himself.*

*Bob loved and trusted Michelle and me throughout the entire disease period. One night when Michelle was visiting, Bob told her she could sleep in Nick's bed, since he wasn't using it. Nick, Bob's roommate, became ill and had been moved to a hospital. Nick later passed away.*

*In December 2005, when Bob was still up to going out for a short car ride, Michelle and I would take him out to see the Christmas lights. One evening when I arrived, Bob spotted me walking through the door of Floral Vale and asked if we were going out for a ride. I said 'Yes'. He sped off to get his coat, while I signed him out.*

*As soon as we were walking to the car, Bob told me that his throat was hurting. I asked him if he had told anyone at Floral Vale about his sore throat, and he said 'No'. We went to the pharmacy and purchased some throat lozenges. He chewed a few of them and said his throat still hurt. Poor guy, he must have thought his throat would improve after consuming just a few lozenges.*

*Bob had a history of bronchitis throughout his adult life. He never had a simple cold. He always developed bronchitis or an upper respiratory infection within days of the first cold symptoms. The next day, Bob was not feeling well, and he spent much of the day in bed. When I saw him that evening, I knew he had to see a doctor before the weekend. The next day was Friday, and Christmas Day was on Sunday. Michelle was able to make an appointment with Bob's primary physician on Friday, and, as expected, Bob was diagnosed with bronchitis.*

*I didn't know if Bob would be feeling well enough to go out on Christmas Day, but he was determined to go. We went to Michelle's house in the afternoon, so Bob could open our gifts to him. After that, we went to my sister and brother-in-law's house for dinner. Bob had been telling the staff at Floral Vale that he was going to his brother-in-law's house for Christmas dinner, and that he was going to have stuffed shells. Bob put in a full day, and he was completely exhausted when Michelle and I finally returned him to Floral Vale.*

*I was off from work the next day, and I went to visit Bob in the morning. He wasn't feeling well; the activities of the previous day had taken a toll and he needed to rest.*

*Bob slowly recovered from the bronchitis, but he had passed a critical turning point in his journey. He never really came back. Bob never again resembled the person we had come to know—the "New Bob." His condition worsened and he lost focus. Bob stopped calling me, which hurt. I missed hearing his voice and knowing that he was thinking of me. The staff at Floral Vale tried to encourage Bob to call me, but he simply couldn't focus.*

*I tried calling Bob, but he wouldn't stay on the phone for more than a minute or so. He would place the phone on the desk, or hand it back to the person at the front desk, or hang up and walk away in mid-sentence. I had to accept the fact that my daily phone calls from Bob were at an end.*

*Bob's interest in food also began to diminish. He was less steady on his feet, and he slept more. In the evening, when I would arrive, Bob typically led me to his room, so we could lie next to each other in his bed. This seemed to comfort him, and I valued every precious moment we had together.*

*As I mentioned earlier, birthdays became very important to Bob. He began to look forward to his fiftieth birthday several months before the event. He told us that he wanted a big party. We thought for several months about how to best celebrate Bob's special day. He became over-stimulated in large crowds, and he tired easily. We decided that two short parties would work best.*

*Michelle made invitations with Bob's photo on them. We gave him his own copy of the invitation and he was thrilled to see his picture! One of the staff members told us that Bob spent time walking around with invitation in hand, inviting other residents to his party. Bob's family came for the lunchtime party. My family and some friends came for the evening party. We thought this would allow time for Bob to take a nap between events.*

*The parties took place the day before Bob's actual birthday. Our guests did a great job of selecting gifts that pleased Bob. He received a new Drexel University jacket and sweatshirt, gift cards, and quite a supply of Skittles and other goodies. Of course, we had no way of knowing that we were celebrating Bob's last birthday. We were just happy at the time that we were able to give him the party he wanted and were able to take photos that we knew we'd cherish the rest of our lives.*

*We got some great pictures of Bob with us and with family members. There were some funny ones, too. We were trying to pose Bob with Michelle, a nephew and two nieces, but Bob was oblivious to what we were trying to accomplish. After all, he had a piece of cake in hand and was eating the icing off it; taking pictures wasn't a priority to him at that point.*

**Michelle:** *A friend of my mom sent Bob a birthday card and included a few scratch off lottery tickets. We held on to the card until his actual birthday. When my mom gave the card to Bob, he opened it and handed the lottery tickets to me and told me to scratch them. One ticket paid off for a dollar. When I told Bob that he had won, he promptly asked, 'So, where it is then?' I reached into my pocket and handed him a one-dollar bill, which he quickly deposited into his wallet. My mom had been in Bob's room putting his clean laundry away during this time and when she returned, I told her that I was glad he hadn't won $1,000—the wait for the cash would have troubled him.*

**Marie:** *A month or so before Bob's birthday, Rita from Floral Vale called to tell me that she had a surprise for us. Floral Vale typically has a family event once a month and Rita was able to schedule the January event for Bob's actual birthday. She had arranged to have a Blues Band come and play that evening and the night was to be a fundraiser for the Association of Frontotemporal Dementias (AFTD), as well as Bob's fiftieth birthday celebration.*

*The evening was a huge success! A donation of more than $300 was made to AFTD, and everyone in attendance had a great time. Bob enjoyed having everyone sing "Happy Birthday" to him, but he spent most of the evening playing a hand-held electronic game that he was given as a gift at his party the day before. The evening went on after Bob's normal bedtime, so when he became tired, I walked him back to his room and tucked him in for the night.*

**Michelle:** *A few weeks later, I took Bob for a scheduled appointment to the neurologist. Dr. Antelo was trying to spark some conversation with Bob. I asked Bob to tell Dr. Antelo about his birthday. As stated before, Bob was still very articulate. He told Dr. Antelo, 'My birthday was on January 23rd. Unfortunately, I didn't have a party or get any gifts.' I said 'Robert James! You had three parties and got lots of gifts.' He said, 'Oh yeah,' and cracked up laughing!*

*Following a hospitalization in January 2006, I was out of work for a few months. During this time, I spent several afternoons with Bob. Our visits were generally short, maybe forty-five minutes to an hour, but one afternoon in February he "let" me stay for well over an hour. I was getting ready to leave, to run a few errands and pick up a prescription at the pharmacy for my mom, when Bob asked, 'Did you want to take me for a car ride?' He badly wanted to get out, so I asked him if he would help me run this errand for my mom. He was always eager to please her, so he readily agreed. The prescription had already been called in to the pharmacy, so we just had to pick it up.*

*When we arrived at the store, we found it decorated for Valentine's Day. I asked Bob if he would like to pick out a card for my mom. He said, 'No, I don't!' I was a bit surprised by this. I asked him if he was sure, and he said, 'Let's just pick up the prescription.' I thought Bob would be excited about getting a Valentine's Day card for my mom. At this point, he was focused on the task at hand. If I had initially mentioned going out for a card, I think he would have been happy to do so, but this wasn't what I had said. This is an example of Bob only being able to process one thought at a time. We went out for a prescription, and that's what we got. I asked him once again, after we had the prescription in our hands, if he would like to choose a card. He said, 'No, take me back to Floral Vale now.'*

**Marie:** *Shortly after Bob's birthday, he began packing. This behavior is typical of dementia patients. Bob wanted to go home. He packed his belongings, including a bouquet of balloons that he got for his birthday, and carried them around all day. This behavior disturbed the staff, and I was eventually asked to take the balloons home. It broke my heart. They were his balloons, and he wasn't hurting anyone with them. Management, however, felt he was becoming obsessed about leaving the facility, and that removing the balloons would discourage that thought. I agreed to give it a try; however, Bob continued to pack his other items of importance.*

*When Bob was well, he loved to read! After Bill Clinton's autobiography had been published, Bob expressed an interest in reading it. At this point, he was losing interest in many of his activities, so I was happy to get the book for him. I don't think Bob even read the entire first chapter, but he enjoyed looking at the pictures. In hindsight, I see that the book was too much of a challenge.*

*Later in the illness, that book remained important to Bob. He would say that he was going to have Bill Clinton sign it the next time he ran into the former president. When Bob moved to Mill Run, we made sure he had the book in his room. When Bob began to pack at Floral Vale, the book was one of the items he would carry around with him.*

*Bob kept a photo album in his room, that included pictures of family and friends. He enjoyed looking through the album and pointing out each individual who appeared in the photos. Michelle and I wrote captions near each picture, including the names of the people in them. We thought that Bob might begin to forget these details and that the captions would be helpful. I'm not sure if Bob had trouble remembering the faces, but eventually when we'd look through the albums together, he had read these captions word-for-word. Knowing the names of the people and places and events seemed to give him confidence. When he looked through the albums, he didn't have to struggle. The information was there for him, and he was able to focus on the enjoyable experience of simply going through the album.*

*One evening in February 2006, when Bob and I were lying in his bed and holding hands, he asked me if he was a good husband. I replied, 'Yes you are, and if there were an Olympics for the Best Husband, you would win a gold medal!' Without a moment's hesitation he asked, 'Better than Mike Stafford?' (my first husband). I was shocked by this question, but reassured him by saying, 'There is no comparison, and you are the best husband for me and the best father to Michelle.' He asked, 'I am?' And I answered, 'Yes, you are; we love you very much.' He said, 'That's good.' We had this conversation a few more times before Bob was admitted to the hospital in March. I always answered his questions the same way.*

*Bob would routinely change into his pajamas and get into bed for the night. Before I left, I would tuck him in and kiss him good night, and then he would say, 'Turn out the light before you leave.' The light switch was near the door, and I would always look back at him and say, 'Good night, honey. I love you. I'll see you next time'. I would blow him a kiss, turn out the light, and close the door behind me.*

*He was becoming more confused which became more noticeable during my evening visits. Bob had been a computer programmer and business analyst and had worked with financial systems. One night when we were lying in bed and holding hands as usual, he told me that he had been on the phone for a long time that day. I asked, 'You were?' He said, 'Yes, I had a big computer problem to fix and it took a long time.' Knowing this couldn't be true, I asked, 'Did you get the problem fixed?' He answered, 'Yes, I did!' I said, 'You must feel so much better now knowing that has been taken care of.' He said, 'Yes, I do.' I felt such sadness knowing that this was the type of thing he had once done so well. Now it was only a faint memory, just a flashback for him.*

*Another night, while we were lying in bed, Bob said something about a boat. We were not boat or water people, so I had no idea what he was talking about. In an effort to try to draw him out, I asked, 'Who was on the boat?' He said, 'William Shatner.' I had to smile. Bob had always been a Star Trek fan, and for him to think of William Shatner was meaningful. I said, 'Oh, so William Shatner was on a boat?' He said, 'Yes,' and then he struggled with his next words. He said, 'William Shatner's on the Tri—tranic.' He was trying to say, William Shatner was on the Titanic. I have no idea why he was thinking about a boat, but since he was, he sure came up with a famous one!*

*Bob's wedding ring was always important to him, and its importance continued throughout the illness. Our matching wedding bands have three small diamonds in them. Bob would frequently tell me, 'This is my wedding ring.' I would answer, 'Yes it is, and I have one that matches.' Then he would say, 'There are three diamonds in it— one for each of us.' He was referring to me, Michelle, and himself. He related the same story to staff members.*

*On another visit, just a few weeks before Bob entered the hospital, he was adjusting his wedding band. Again, he told me about the three diamonds and what they represented to him. We were lying in bed holding hands. I told Bob I loved him, and he gave me a few small kisses. Then he looked at me and said, 'We should get married!' I usually tried not to correct Bob, but this time I felt a need to do so. I said, 'Honey, we're already married.' He responded with, 'No, I said we should get married.' I simply said, 'OK.'*

*I realized Bob must have thought that I hadn't understood him or that perhaps I wasn't listening closely. A sad but sweet moment. Sad because he didn't remember we were married, but sweet because he still wanted to be married to me.*

# CHAPTER NINE

## FINAL DAYS

The end of the journey is marked by the family's sense that the afflicted family member is dying, and death seems imminent. Previously effective medical treatments now seem to bring only temporary improvements. Family members face an inescapable reality: the beloved family member is not coming back, life is ending. The dementia journey is nearing an end.

This end-of-life phase evokes a mix of feelings: sadness and grief, sometimes coupled with a sense of relief. It also presents two major challenges:

- How to ensure a "good death" for the afflicted family member.
- How to help with closure for caregivers and other family members.

**Marie**: *In early March, Bob began to display cold-like symptoms; the staff was aware of how quickly he had developed bronchitis in December. So, on Friday, March 10, 2006, Betty, the Director of Floral Vale, called me to discuss Bob's symptoms. She suggested that I call his primary care physician to inquire about the need for some medications that would nip the infection. Betty was concerned because the weekend was approaching, and if the condition worsened, she feared that Bob would be unable to get needed attention until the next Monday.*

*Bob's doctor called in a prescription, and I made an appointment for Monday, March 13, 2006. Once again, Bob was diagnosed with bronchitis. At the doctor's office, we were able to weigh him, and we learned that he'd lost more weight in the preceding two weeks. I wasn't surprised. He'd been eating very little and was beginning to look very thin.*

*I visited Bob briefly the next day, Tuesday. He wasn't feeling well and was in bed, fully clothed, when I arrived. Bob said he didn't want to change into pajamas. The next day I found him sitting in an easy chair in one of the living rooms, sound asleep. He didn't look well; he was sleeping soundly, with his mouth open and his head back. I gently tried to wake him, but he didn't respond. I was worried, and I sent a text message to Michelle on her cell phone conveying my concern. She offered to come right over.*

*In the meantime, the concierge spotted us and asked if Bob was OK. She, too, was unable to wake him. She summoned the Care Manager, who shook Bob's shoulder and loudly called his name. Bob awoke and stumbled to his room.*

*He found his pajamas and went into the bathroom, leaving the door slightly ajar. I could hear him struggling, so I looked in. I could see that he had gotten his jeans down to his ankles, without unzipping them or unbuckling his belt. He was sitting on the toilet seat, unsure about what to do next. I walked in and said, 'I see the problem and I can help.' I gently removed the jeans and helped him put on his pajama bottoms. He had successfully put on the pajama top.*

*By the time Michelle arrived, Bob was already in bed. He just wanted to fall asleep. He asked me to turn off the lights, and I did.*

*I called the next morning, and Betty said, 'Bob is looking a little better this morning. He is dressed; he ate breakfast and has been spending time in Town Square.' I was relieved.*

*I had a dentist appointment that evening and could not visit, but Michelle offered to check in. She called and gave me a good report. Bob had eaten dinner (quickly, as usual) and had seemed more alert. We were both encouraged.*

*On Friday, I called Betty and learned that Bob wasn't doing well. Betty said that she would observe him throughout the day and monitor his progress. She also said that she would be the manager on duty over the weekend and would keep a close eye on him.*

*I visited Bob on Saturday, and was struck by his tired and frail appearance. He was waiting for me in Town Square. I had brought water ice, a treat that we enjoyed together, and then Bob went to his room to rest. I told Betty I was scheduled to work on Sunday afternoon and would not be visiting, but I would call in the morning for an update. When I called, I learned that Bob had eaten some breakfast but appeared lethargic. Staff members had been trying to give him fluids to avoid dehydration. Betty suggested that he see his primary care physician again on Monday.*

*I arrived at work by noon on Sunday. An hour or so later, Michelle called me for an update on Bob. At that time she asked, 'Why wait until tomorrow to see the doctor? If Bob is that sick, Dr. Dunn will tell you to take him to the hospital.' Michelle offered to call Betty and make the arrangements to get Bob to the emergency room. This made sense.*

*When Michelle spoke with Betty, she learned that Bob's breathing had become shallow and that he'd agreed to take some oxygen. This information affirmed that we had made the right decision. On Sunday evening, March 19, 2006, Michelle and I took Bob to the St. Mary Medical Center Emergency Room. The receptionist took one look at Bob and said, 'You should have called an ambulance so he wouldn't have had to wait.' The staff quickly began attending to Bob.*

*Even in his weakened condition, Bob could not sit still for long. I walked around the room with him, arm in arm. When we approached the entrance to the emergency room, the doors would open automatically, and Bob would then want to go outside. It was a dark and cold night, and I would say, 'We can't go out. I don't have my coat.' After the fifth time I'd given him this excuse, he said, 'Then why don't you put your coat on?' This was so typical of Bob, always solving problems, right up to the end.*

*The triage nurse examined Bob and took the required medical information from me. She then arranged for Bob to have a chest x-ray. Bob, Michelle, and I walked to the x-ray department in the emergency room. The technician commented that she knew Bob from somewhere, but I couldn't imagine where she would have met him. It turned out she knew him from Floral Vale. She would occasionally take x-rays of residents there, and Bob as unofficial greeter had become a familiar face.*

*The emergency room setting frightened Bob. We were taken to a room within the ER, and Bob was asked to change into a hospital gown. He had absolutely no interest in taking off his coat and removing his clothes. Michelle told him that she was going to take a walk and stepped out of the room, thinking that her absence would make him feel more comfortable.*

*I explained to Bob the need to remove his coat so he could change into the hospital gown. Bob had other ideas, one of which was to get out of that room, with his coat still ON. He managed to exit the room, and as I struggled to return him, a nurse came by and noticed the problem. She spoke gently to Bob, and he cooperated with her; allowing the two of us to get him changed and into a bed.*

*The next few hours seemed like a blur however I do remember a few things. A nurse came in and started an IV and then a doctor came in to ask health-related questions. All the while, Michelle and I were struggling to keep Bob in bed, trying to distract him and keep him from pulling on the IV and other apparatus. Bob kept taking the oxygen tube from inside his nose and placing it on the bridge, where eyeglasses normally sit. The oxygen was blowing directly into his eyes, causing them to blink frequently. Each time we put the tube back in Bob's nostrils, it would only remain there a short time before he moved it again.*

*Bob was hooked up to a telemetry unit that monitored his vital signs. It was color coded with dots, for the placement of the EKG leads. Bob began "playing a video game" with the unit. He was watching the TV screen and pressing the color-coded dots on the unit. Michelle asked Bob how the game was going, but he was so immersed in it that he didn't reply. Michelle and I smiled; we appreciated his creativity. He seemed content with the way he was passing time, as we awaited the lab results.*

*Bob was finally diagnosed with pneumonia and admitted to St. Mary Medical Center sometime around midnight. He had a dedicated one-on-one nurse because of his dementia. After getting him settled in a room and taking his vitals, the nurse spent time with me, attempting to gain an understanding of the dementia level and the degree of remaining capabilities. I answered her questions as best as I could, and I then told Bob that the nurse would be with him through the night. I told him Michelle and I were leaving. I hugged Bob and kissed him and told him I would see him the next day. I arrived home at approximately 1:00 a.m.*

*I called the hospital the next morning, Monday, and the nurse told me that Bob hadn't slept much and again seemed lethargic. I told her that he had been lethargic for some time. She replied, 'He is very lethargic.' I told her I would come after lunch, when visiting hours began.*

*At 1:00 p.m. Dr. Shah called to tell me that Bob had stopped breathing, had been placed on a ventilator and was on his way to the Intensive Care Unit. I told him I would be there shortly. I called Michelle, who was on her way to my house. When she arrived, we hugged and sobbed. I remember saying, 'This can't be happening. God didn't prepare me for this.' My house was only a half-mile from the hospital, and we quickly arrived.*

*I walked into the Intensive Care Unit, Room #3, to see several staff members caring for Bob. There he was, my precious husband, lying there with his eyes closed, hooked up to a ventilator, and sprouting more IVs than I had ever seen. I went to him, took his hand and I told him I loved him. I explained to Bob that he was in St. Mary's and that he had pneumonia. I told him he was very sick but that the doctors and nurses were taking good care of him. I know Bob heard me, I could see his eyes filling up with tears. I continued talking, and I did my best to lean over the bars on the bed and kiss his cheek.*

## Final Days

*Although Bob had a Living Will, having him on the ventilator was not considered to be life support at this point because he was on it to help him recover from pneumonia. The goal was to have him weaned from the ventilator by Friday (this was Monday). That sounded encouraging, but at the same time I was scared to death.*

*The day passed in a blur. Michelle and I talked to Bob and asked him to open his eyes or to squeeze our hands. There was no response. Bob's parents; Betty, the Director of Floral Vale; Bob's brother, Tom; and our friend, Linda, all came to the hospital that day.*

*I didn't want to leave Bob that night. I thought he might wake up and become frightened. I was afraid of the unknown. Plus, I knew Bob would never leave my side if I were lying in that hospital bed instead of him. Tom encouraged me to go home and get some sleep. He told me that I had to take care of myself. He said, 'You live less than five minutes away. Ask the nurse to call you right away if anything changes.' I took his advice and returned home.*

*From that night on, Michelle stayed with me at my house. She wanted to be nearby in the event we received any emergency calls. We comforted and supported each other.*

*Whenever I was with Bob, I always talked to him in a normal fashion, always assuming that he could comprehend everything I was saying. I tried my best to explain what was happening. I told him about family and friends who were sending their love and prayers. The first week on the ventilator, my words would bring tears to Bob's eyes. It was sad, and yet comforting at the same time. Sad that he was going through this difficult time, but comforting to know that he understood I was there.*

*Before leaving his room, I would tell Bob why I was leaving and when I would return. If the nurse, for example, needed a few minutes with Bob, to suction and turn him, I would say, 'Honey, I'm going to step out of the room for a few minutes while the nurse tries to make you comfortable. I'll be back as soon as she is finished.' Then when I returned, I would go to him and tell him I was back.*

*From that day forward our world took many twists and turns. On Tuesday, March 21, Bob had a good day. His chest x-ray showed slight improvement, and the respiratory people were able to reduce the oxygen volume.*

*On Wednesday, medical staff tried to wean Bob from the ventilator. He did well for an hour, and then had a seizure, which set him back.*

*On Thursday, we were told that Bob had had a bad night. A CAT scan showed that he had aspirated during the seizure, so a bronchoscopy was performed that morning. He then rested comfortably the rest of the day, but it was clear that Bob had a tough road ahead. Occasionally, we'd see his eyes flicker for a moment, but he was unable to respond to us.*

*Friday was initially thought to be the day Bob would be totally weaned from the ventilator. Unfortunately, this was not to be as a result of his set backs that week.*

*On Saturday, he awoke for the first time. Michelle and I were at his bedside and he seemed to recognize us. We were thrilled!*

*On Sunday morning, Bob was taken off the ventilator for almost five hours. He slept most of the day; we think the lack of ventilator assistance exhausted him. We were told by the medical staff that they were hoping to take him off the ventilator in the coming days, but that he would remain in the ICU for a day or two afterwards. He would then be moved to a step-down unit.*

*Bob was very weak at this point. We still didn't know whether the seizure had affected his brain in any way. It had been an exhausting week.*

*Michelle continued to be an unending source of support. She continued to stay with me, at my house. With her experience as a hospital pharmacist, she was able to explain medical information to me when I had questions. She drove me to and from the hospital. She was a blessing and a tremendous pillar on which to lean.*

*Bob was able to go off the ventilator for several hours on one particular day, but the next day did not go well. On two occasions, he had to be resuscitated while ventilator weaning attempts were being made.*

*He ultimately spent nineteen days in the Intensive Care Unit at St. Mary Medical Center. Some days, we received encouraging news, while other days, it didn't seem as though he would survive the week. On Monday, March 23, I sent this e-mail to close friends:*

> The pneumonia is improving but Bob is very weak. The medical staff continues to give us hope that Bob will pull through. They have been asking me questions about his typical behavior, trying to get a baseline about what they can expect from him.

*On Tuesday, Dr. Solomon, one of Bob's pulmonary doctors, came to speak with us. He explained that it is not in the patient's best interest to be intubated (a tube through the mouth) on a ventilator for more than ten to fourteen days because the tube stretches the vocal cords. When taken off of the ventilator Bob might have trouble speaking. While intubated, Bob had a tube that ran through his nose into his stomach to enable him to be nourished with tube feedings. Dr. Solomon explained the option of inserting a trach (a tube through the throat) and then a feeding tube into the stomach. He also explained that the procedure isn't as invasive as it sounds and would be better for Bob in the long term. He asked us to think about this option and said he would check with us later in the week. If we decided to have the trach inserted, the ventilator would continue to assist Bob with breathing. The only change would be the placement of the tube into Bob's body.*

*I didn't know what to think. I knew Bob had a Living Will, with instructions not to put him on life support. I kept asking myself, 'What constitutes life support?' The social worker explained that I could limit the number of days I wanted Bob on the trach if I chose that option. It was all overwhelming and confusing. Some days we saw reasons to be hopeful; other days it just seemed as though Bob faced too many challenges.*

*Approximately ten days after Bob had been admitted to the ICU, the pulmonary doctor told us that Bob was recovering from pneumonia and didn't need to be in ICU anymore as a way of treating the pneumonia. Dr. Solomon said that Bob was now on the ventilator because of neurological changes. He had daily x-rays and routine CAT scans. Bob also had an MRI to rule out a stroke. The doctors had stopped the antibiotics and most other medications, hoping this would lower his ammonia level, which they thought might be preventing him from waking up. The medical staff initially thought Bob's ammonia level was high due to a side effect from a medication he was on while in the hospital. Once the medication was discontinued and his ammonia levels were back within normal limits, Bob still did not respond.*

*On Wednesday, March 29, I visited Bob by myself as Michelle had an appointment. When I entered the room, Bob's appearance startled me. His eyes were wide open, but there was no recognition of his surroundings or me. I knew in my heart that this was the beginning of the end.*

*I began to talk to Bob, telling him how happy I was to see him with his eyes open. I kissed him and tried to hug him but I finally broke down and began sobbing. I knew, I just knew that we were going to finally lose him to this horrendous invader— this dementia.*

*On Tuesday, April 4, Dr. Solomon met with Michelle and me to ask if we had made a decision about the trach. I asked Dr. Solomon, 'At what point does the ventilator constitute life support?,' and I explained that Bob had a Living Will. Dr. Solomon said, 'Now that I know Bob has a Living Will, let me take the responsibility for that decision off your shoulders. I have a moral obligation to follow Bob's wishes.'*

*We decided to take Bob off the ventilator on the coming Friday. This would give us a few days and allow family members to make their last visits.*

*On Wednesday, Michelle suggested I contact the funeral home to make funeral arrangements. On Thursday morning, we met with the funeral home director to plan Bob's funeral.*

*That evening we met with Pastor Weleck, who helped prepare us for Bob's death. He explained to us what we could expect and shared some very important information. In his experience, he found that sometimes the dying wait for family members to arrive, before passing on. Others wait for loved ones to leave the room. These words saved us from unnecessary grief and guilt later.*

*Michelle and I stayed with Bob until about midnight on Thursday. I sat beside him holding his hand. I had been trying to leave for two hours, but couldn't seem to pull myself away. Finally, shortly before midnight, I knew I had to go home and get some sleep, because the next day would be difficult. I wanted to spend as much time with Bob as I could. Michelle and I took turns spending time alone with him, speaking from our hearts, sharing our feelings, and telling him how much we loved him. I thanked Bob for being a wonderful husband and father. I told him that he was very sick, and that if he was too tired to continue fighting for his life, it was OK to let go. I said that Michelle and I would take care of each other; I would always love him and he would remain in my heart forever.*

*The next day, Friday, April 7, 2006, Michelle and I arrived at the hospital in the morning, in order to have some time with Bob. I told him that the doctors were going to remove the ventilator, the IVs and do everything they could to make him comfortable. I told him I loved him and that I would miss him. I also repeated all the things I'd told him the night before.*

*Pastor Weleck was due to arrive at 11:30 a.m. to give Bob his last rites. Bob's parents and brothers Tom, John, and Steve also came to be with Bob. Last rites were administered, and the physician arrived. I signed the paper authorizing the removal of the ventilator.*

*At approximately 2:30 p.m. Bob was taken off the vent, his breathing stayed shallow, and he did not appear to be struggling in any way. A few hours later, I noticed that his fingernails were turning blue, but his fingers remained white, and he still retained good color in his face. It had been a long day for everyone, and we had no idea how long he would hold on.*

*At approximately 5:30 p.m., Michelle and I, along with Bob's brother Tom, went to the cafeteria to grab a sandwich. We planned then to return to Bob's room to allow Bob's parents and brother, John, to go to the cafeteria. Steve had left the hospital.*

*At 5:40 p.m., John entered the cafeteria. Tom said, 'There's John. Something must be wrong.' John rushed over and said, 'Dad said it looks like something is changing and to come quick.' We rushed back to the ICU.*

*When we arrived, Bob had passed away, with his parents by his side. When I looked at him, I gasped. He was completely white. Only fifteen minutes earlier he had color in his face. Bob's mother said that he had passed peacefully. I was thankful that he was not alone when he took his last breath.*

*Michelle and I were sobbing and hugging Bob, when Michelle said to me, 'Mom, he waited for us to leave. He didn't want us to be here when this happened.' I immediately thought about the conversation with Pastor Weleck the night before. I truly believe that Bob waited for us to leave the room before leaving this life.*

# CHAPTER TEN

# SOME REFLECTIONS

We tend to think of death as an entirely unwelcome event. For many family members, the notion of a "good death" may seem strange. In recent years, millions of Americans have expressed interest in a "good death," an end-of-life experience that focuses on comfort and dignity and adherence to previously stated wishes. A "good death" for the impaired loved one, then, should be a death where end-of-life decisions have been in keeping with the patient's wishes and values.

Even with a "good death," closure for families who have lost a loved one to dementia is a difficult and complex issue. Closure for the family involves not only a "goodbye" to the loved one but also a "letting go" of the illness.

**Marie:** *We learned there is so much more to Frontotemporal Dementia than the disease itself. There are so many other* *pressures and worries. Our hearts have been broken over and over again. In attempting to obtain a diagnosis, I hit one brick wall after another. At the time, Bob was compensating well. His illness was difficult to diagnose. Moreover, because of his relatively young age, he didn't qualify for many helpful programs. One adult care facility and nursing home told me that they couldn't accept Bob because he was too mobile and, except for the dementia, too healthy. They felt he was a "flight risk."*

*The dementia experience has been described as a long goodbye—and indeed it is. This cruel disease strips a victim of dignity and pride, of the ability to live a reasonable and self-sufficient life. Up until the time Bob stopped breathing, and went on the ventilator, he recognized us. He could dress himself, make his bed, and take care of his personal needs. Had he lived longer, the dementia would surely have robbed him of these capabilities and would have stripped away even more of his dignity and sense of self.*

*Bob passed away much sooner than we ever expected, his body ravaged by the disease, his quality of life largely destroyed. I find comfort in knowing that it could have been worse. God spared Bob the loss of even more dignity and spared those who loved him from having to helplessly watch. It doesn't lessen our pain, nor does it cause us to miss him any less. Indeed, I'm finding that I miss Bob more and more as time goes by.*

*Nonetheless, I remember telling visitors at Bob's viewing that it was more painful to watch Bob suffer the effects of dementia than it was to let him go, when the time came. Even with the loss, I find comfort in the knowledge that this good man no longer has to endure this brutal disease. Had he lived longer, he could have reached a point that he would no longer recognize us, and he may have developed an extreme dependency on others. My heart aches, and I want him back. I want the "Old Bob," the healthy Bob, but it was not meant to be.*

*At the viewing, a friend Margie said to me, 'You were very fortunate to have had such love in the eighteen years you were married. Some people don't experience that over an entire lifetime.' What an eye opening statement!*

*I feel that Bob was cheated, and we were cheated; we were not allowed to grow old together. It is hard to think about the milestones and events that lie ahead for Michelle—marriage, maybe children some day—and to know that Bob won't share in that happiness. What we had for eighteen years was so special, and I feel his presence in my heart. He is truly with both me and Michelle.*

*One day, the "New Bob" asked me if he was going to walk Michelle down the aisle when she got married. His disease was advancing, and I knew that such an event would not be an option. I didn't know how to answer. I thought I could redirect him by saying, 'I don't know. You will have to ask Michelle that question.' And, to my surprise, he did ask Michelle, and it was a touching and loving question.*

*Throughout this journey, Bob, Michelle, and I were blessed over and over by an outpouring of love, support, and concern. Family and friends expressed their feelings of helplessness. They wanted to help; it was just hard for them to know exactly what to do. Just knowing they cared about us and were praying for us gave us strength and fortitude.*

*Our primary goals for Bob were to keep him safe and to preserve his dignity. At a certain point in the disease, Michelle and I started referring to Bob as the "Old Bob" and the "New Bob." Letting go of the "Old Bob," the man we knew and loved for so many years, was painful, but the disease gave us no other option. Fortunately, with time, we grew to know and love* the *"New Bob,"* with his childlike innocence. We truly loved *"both" Bobs.*

*On October 18, 2006, I wrote the following note to a coworker who had expressed concern about me. The words sum up where I was at that point in my mourning process.*

Thank you for your concern about me. All things considered, I'm doing well. I have my moments, but I learned so much about myself while going through the journey.

I began to lose my husband in the true sense of the word even before he was diagnosed. Then, having to watch this once intelligent man, who was the "rock" in my life, regress into a child was heartbreaking. I lived every day knowing that this is as good as it gets for Bob. Change always resulted in more decline. I was truly blessed by his love, and that helped give me strength to get through those painful days.

A month or so after Bob passed away a friend wrote the following message, "You always said the only thing Bob ever wanted was for you to be happy. The best way for you to honor Bob is to do just that—be happy and live life to the fullest." Those words have helped me so much!

I miss him very much, but had he lived longer, he would have lost even more of his dignity. I feel God spared Bob from having to endure this additional loss and, as a result, He also spared those of us who love him.

Thank you for caring and for "listening".

Marie

*nice Poem*

## Poem on the back of Bob's prayer card.

" God saw you getting tired and a cure was not to be.
He put His arms around you and whispered, "Come to Me."
With tearful eyes we watched you, and saw you pass away.
Although we loved you dearly, we could not make you stay.
A golden heart stopped beating, hard working hands at rest.
God broke our hearts to prove to us, He only takes the best. "

# CHAPTER ELEVEN

# REMEMBRANCES AND RECOLLECTIONS

**M**arie: *Some of Bob's best qualities are best described by friends. The following notes and expressions of condolences have been of great help to both me and Michelle. Thanks one and all for your love and support.*

> "It is said that everyone brightens a room, some by entering, and some by leaving. Bob was one of those who always brightened a room by entering.
>
> With his always beaming smile, and love of puns (the worse they were, the more he liked them), he was a charming gentleman, always welcome in any gathering. Everyone's biggest memory of Bob will be his laugh. He liked to laugh – richly, deeply, and often. So, Bob, thank you for sharing your many gifts, your talent, your energy, and your love of life!"
>
> – Dave Peters

"One visit in particular stands out in my mind. We had been talking about a behavior of Bob's, when Marie explained to him that he couldn't do "that" anymore. She asked Bob, 'Do you understand why you can't do that?' And he answered, 'Because I love you?' Bob didn't understand why he couldn't continue this behavior, but he knew he loved Marie.'

– Dr. Ronny Antelo, Neurologist

"My first thought and memory was of all the greeting cards Bob had saved from his dear friends and family members. You had these at his funeral service, and someone mentioned to me that he had saved every one. This was so touching. It all comes down to the relationships and love we have for one another, and he got and gave his full share. He was a special soul."

– Susan Selman

"It takes a special man to take on another family and to do so well with them. Michelle, it is obvious by the way you have turned out that he and your Mom did a great job. Of course, this is why you were able to do such a good job with him in his need. You learned from him. You both were so blessed to have had him during important years of your lives."

– Anne Mauro

"The thing I remember most about the "New Bob" was how much he enjoyed all of the things that the two of you had done together. He loved to talk about the cruise and the trip to London. He would have a big grin on his face whenever he talked about it.

The thing I remember most about the "Old Bob" was what good care he took of you. I remember you telling me how he would iron your clothes for work and bring you a cup of tea in the morning."

– Denice Barnes

"My memory of Bob is his unique laugh and his excitement at telling or showing pictures of your trips. I also remember the time we discovered that he liked music. He would come out and turn up the radio by the front desk. One day, he kept turning the volume up louder and louder. Then he started dancing and singing along. At one point, he had it so loud that Jen could not hear the person on the other end of the phone. He would tell her, "It's OK, have some fun.""

– Betty Moran-Organ

"I have thought about Bob, and I remember always a smile, a gentle man, and a gentleman. He was always there to help or listen, someone who always made you feel comfortable.

The "Old Bob" was so gracious and proud on the day Michelle graduated from pharmacy school. He seemed to just about "pop his buttons" the entire day. I thought his expressions clearly indicated his feelings for Michelle."

– Dottie Fenimore

Michelle's Graduation from the University of the Sciences in Philadelphia, May 1999

# Sykes Family Photo Album

*Bobby outside of his Grandparents' (Hoehn) Bakery*

*Bobby at Grandmom's*

*Kathy, "Big" Bob and Tom*

*(Top) Bob, (L to R) Cousin Karen, Kathy, Tom, Cousin Rusty, (Bottom) John*

*Our wedding day*

*Bob with his niece and Goddaughter, Vickie*

*Bob, Marie and Santa*

*Bob and Tom serving as Usher's at John's Wedding*

*Marie and Bob on the Spirit of Philadelphia*

*Michelle and Bob before Steve's Wedding*

*Marie and Bob at home*

*Bob with his favorite Disney character, Goofy!*

*One of Marie's favorite pictures of Bob*

*Bermuda – June 2002*

*Bob at Peddler's Village, Lahaska, PA – October 2005*

# Bob's 50th Birthday
## January 23, 2006

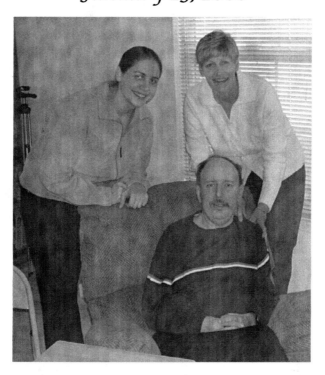

*An Evolution of Love*

*Bob with his Parents*

$\mathcal{T}$hank you for reading our story.

$\mathcal{F}$or each book sold, a donation will be made to –

The Association of Frontotemporal Dementias (AFTD)

$\mathcal{W}$e invite you to visit our website:

www.AnEvolutionOfLove.com

Printed in the United States
130350LV00010B/152/P

9 780615 154497